A Lot Like Eve

A Lot Like Eve

Fashion, Faith and Fig-Leaves:
A memoir

Joanna Jepson

B L O O M S B U R Y
LONDON • NEW DELHI • NEW YORK • SYDNEY

Bloomsbury Continuum
An imprint of Bloomsbury Publishing Plc

50 Bedford Square	1385 Broadway
London	New York
WC1B 3DP	NY 10018
UK	USA

www.bloomsbury.com

Bloomsbury, Continuum and the Diana logo are trademarks of Bloomsbury Publishing Plc

First published 2015

© Joanna Jepson, 2015

British Library Cataloguing in Publication Data
A catalogue record for this book is available from the British Library.

ISBN PB: 9781472913173
ePub: 9781472913180
ePDF: 9781472913197

10 9 8 7 6 5 4 3 2 1

Typeset by Fakenham Prepress Solutions, Fakenham, Norfolk NR21 8NN
Printed and bound in Great Britain by CPI Group (UK) Ltd, Croydon CR0 4YY

To find out more about our authors and books visit www.bloomsbury.com. Here you will find extracts, author interviews, details of forthcoming events and the option to sign up for our newsletters.

For Mum and Dad,
with love

And for all the women and men
in the Community at Ty Mawr

Muddy

'The glory of God is a human being fully alive'
(St Irenaeus)

And so to be children, growing
younger into our humanity.
Born between thorn and nail,
we must live now, here –
eyes wide amid the hurting;
daring to find a love
deep in the poison garden,
learning our steps in the barefoot way,
dancing muddy into eternity.

Patrick Hobbs

Contents

Contents

In the Beginning ...

Paraphrased from Genesis, Chapters 1, 2 and 3.

God said, "Let us make people in our image, in our likeness, and let them tend the earth and every creature in it."

God took some of the dust of the ground and breathed the breath of life into this creature and called him Adam. God took the man to the Garden of Eden, a place of delight and bliss, so that he could work in it and care for it, telling him, "You are free to eat from any tree in the garden; except the Tree of the Knowledge of Good and Evil: you must not eat the fruit of that tree for when you eat of it you will surely die."

But God saw the man alone and realized that this was not good, and so God said, "I will make someone to partner with you fully." Yet none of the animals and creatures were suitable. And so, making the man fall into deep sleep, God took one of the man's ribs and from this rib he shaped and breathed life into a woman. When God brought the woman to him the man recognized her: that he belonged with her and could rely on her and flourish with her.

And this is how God created human beings, breathing life into them, creating them male and female so that together they would reflect God. They were naked and it was good, without shame or fear. Then God blessed them and told them to flourish as they cared for the world and all that was in it.

God looked over all that was created and it was very good, and so, on the seventh day when all creation was complete, God rested.

But there was a sly and devious creature, a serpent who wanted to sow doubt and division into the harmony of the garden, and so he asked the woman, "Did God really say that you mustn't eat from any tree in the garden?"

The woman answered, "We may eat the fruit of the trees in the garden, but God said not to eat the fruit from the tree that's in the middle of the garden – we mustn't even touch that – or we will die."

And even though God hadn't said that they mustn't touch it, the doubt sowed by the serpent was beginning to work its poison … Soon the woman's doubts would alienate her trust in God, and God would be alienated from her: made out to be her accuser.

Swiftly the serpent delivered a blatant blow of untruth. "You will not surely die … for God knows that when you eat of it your eyes will be opened, and you will be like God, knowing good and evil."

It was a promising prospect, and looking again at the fruit, the woman saw that it looked ripe and delicious. So she took some and ate it. Then turning to Adam she gave some to him too, and he also ate it.

At that moment their eyes were opened. But it wasn't anything like the serpent had suggested. They realized they were naked and the shame was unbearable. So, reaching for fig leaves, they wove coverings for themselves.

Later that day they heard the sound of God walking in the garden and so they hid, taking cover from his sight in the thick of the trees. But God missed them and called out to Adam, "Where are you?"

Adam called back, "I heard you in the garden and I was afraid because … because I'm naked; and so I hid."

God asked him, "Who told you that you were naked? How could you know that? Unless … have you eaten the fruit I told you not to?"

*

The game is up. There's nothing he can do to hide any more – except blame the woman and blame God for putting the woman there. So in *fear and desperation Adam tries to deflect, "The woman you put here with me – she gave me the fruit and so I ate it."*

God turns to the woman, "What is this that you've done?"

And she too, feeling cornered, retorts, "It was the serpent! The serpent deceived me and I ate."

God turns to the serpent, "Cursed are you beyond all creatures and animals! You will crawl on your belly and eat dust for the rest of your life. And I will make you and the woman and her children and your offspring to be enemies. They will crush your head and you will strike their heel."

God looks at the woman and says to her, "I will increase your pains in childbearing; with pain you will give birth. You will desire and long for your husband, and he will rule over you."

To Adam, God explains, "Because you listened to your wife and ate from the tree that I told you not to, the ground you work will be cursed. It will demand all your strength to produce the harvest you need. There will be difficulties and toil, thistles and thorns that you will have to overcome. You will sweat in your pursuit of the food you need until the day you die and return to the ground from which you came, for dust you are and to dust you will return."

And then God makes warm garments out of animal skins for Adam and Eve, and he clothes them.

Prologue

There was a uniform for these kinds of occasions. That much I knew. It wasn't something that I was used to wearing and, as I smoothed my hand nervously over the soft suede – checking that it absolutely did cover my backside – I flinched at the drops of rain soaking into the fabric. Despite the puddles of November rain glistening orange beneath the glow of the street lights, the street still looked cold and inhospitable, the bright shop windows invading the blackness of a lonely High Street shut down for the night, indifferent to the temptations on offer. I'd obeyed the crude rules as far as I knew them, dismissing the multitude of long, floral skirts and comfy jeans hanging in my wardrobe until I found the only thing that would meet the requirement: a damson suede mini-skirt. Paired with a Lycra bodysuit that stretched over my curveless frame I had assessed my reflection in the mirror earlier: short skirt: *check*. tight top: *check*. stilettos: groan. My belief that high heels should be confined to weddings and the catwalk was compromised by a pair of high-heeled Mary Janes. The whole ensemble felt like a chore, a collusion with the regulations set out for seventeen-year-old girls, and completely impractical ones at that, I thought, as I grabbed the skimpiest jacket I owned and headed out to the bus stop.

Those who'd devised the uniform weren't thinking of our wellbeing when they dictated that we wear as little as possible on a rainy November night. They weren't thinking about the queue in which we'd stand, freezing, as we tried to curve round into the sheltered alley in front of Marks and Spencer's emergency fire exit doors, our bare legs mottled purple from the cold. It was all about the paradise above: where the disco balls sparkled and flashes of strobes dazzled the punters clamouring for space on the dance floor. Where music obliterated all angst about mock exams, and lurid colours would disguise the blueish hue of my thighs with their shifting shades. This is what it was for: The promised land of cocktails and flirtation. Where I would be transformed from mousy and timid into sassy and kissable.

As the rain began to drizzle down the lank strands of my self-cut fringe I looked up at the blacked-out windows and felt the muffled pounding of the dance anthem behind them, the thumping beat at odds with the panicked beat of my heart.

I'm seventeen and queuing – no, longing – to get into TIME nightclub, and I'm terrified. The queue shuffles forward towards the corded red rope that stands between us and the enveloping heat of hundreds of dancing bodies at the top of the stairs. Being under age is neither here nor there; I have put off this moment for too long. Schoolfriends had been frequenting Smokey Joe's and other clubs since we were fifteen. If I was to survive with a place among my peers I had to make my way through this rite of passage and emerge the other side, accepted and validated.

Even in heels my best friend, Jane, and her schoolfriends were all at least half a foot shorter than me, which made hiding at the back kind of tricky. I also soon saw that it was a downright bad plan. As the girls were waved in two by two I suddenly realized what this would mean: that it would be just Jane and me, and our fake ID.

But that wasn't the worst thing. It wasn't putting that shiny little card with its casually rearranged DOB to the test, nor was it fear of being asked by the bouncer what my date of birth was and having to calmly retort with a lie.

Because I knew that it wasn't the fake ID that was being put to the test. It was my face.

Jane stepped towards the taller bouncer and without flinching looked at him defiantly, daring him to question her credentials. But Jane, once described by a boy as the nearest thing to perfection that he'd ever seen, possessed credentials that would never be challenged. The bouncer, still gazing at Jane, lifted the rope across for her to pass by. I silently begged her to just keep eyeballing him long enough for me to slip past unnoticed but the other bouncer stepped in front of me, and, staring at my face, cut me off from the shelter of Jane's beauty.

I held up my ID but without bothering to even look at it he smirked at his colleague and closed the rope in front of me.

This was it: this was the moment that Jane had coached and prepared me for, the moment where I would confidently shake my hair and muster the flirtatious indignation becoming of a legitimate clubber. But I knew that if I said something there would no longer be any hiding the plastic blocks and metal wires of convoluted orthodontistry that filled my mouth. So I stepped forward instead, trying to affect a silent confidence, challenging his mistake with my bold expectation that I would gain entry. But he shook his head and turned to Jane. "Not her."

'Not her?'

I am relegated to the third person; not even dignified with a refusal to my face. Instinctively I set my lower jaw into the most pronounced under-bite I could muster, hoping those few milli-metres would be mistaken for normality, but the bone-chilling wind had already set my teeth chattering and as I strained my jaw forward I felt the sting of my teeth breaking into my lip.

Jane turned back and grabbed the wrist of the taller bouncer, her eyes flashing wild and alive with indignation.

"What's the problem? She's with us."

The taller bouncer, clearly enjoying Jane's attempt to reach out, smiled cockily at the paunchy one as she continued her protestations.

"You've got to let her in, you've let the rest of us in!"

"She's got ID. What the hell's the matter with you?"

I look to see whether the Jane-effect is having any sway on her wrist-clamped subject but he was laughing. As the other one put out his hand to restrain her she twisted round towards him. But before she could unleash her arguments afresh he moved his head in my direction, stared at my contorted mouth and bleeding lip, then turned back and leant into Jane's face,

"NOT HER."

Within moments our altercation by the rope was overtaken by the group of revellers behind me anxious to get on up into the whirl of TIME's throbbing masses. Stepping back from the rope I dodged my face between their jostling heads so that I could shout to Jane, reassuring her that I'd be fine, that I'd get to the bus stop, that I'd get home okay. Half running down the High Street in my stupid clumpy heels and bedraggled suede skirt, I concentrated on thinking up an excuse to give my parents for having returned so soon after going over to Jane's. I wondered how I would have told them the truth: that I was barred from the one place that could give me the affirmation I was looking for – and that I didn't even qualify to be a wallflower. How could I tell my parents that my face didn't fit – my face literally didn't fit; the bones in my jaws growing out of sync with each other, my teeth protruding so far that hiding was impossible. If we were telling the truth that night – illegal clubbing, under-age drinking and deceiving parents aside – I wonder how they would have refuted the judgement I'd received. I wondered how they would go about digging down to retrieve the ambitions and hopes, inspiration and passions that I had forgotten about myself while standing in front of the rope. How might they have restored me to the vast truth that who I am is so much greater than my misshapen jaws?

But I knew I couldn't tell them the truth. So with aching feet I climbed onto the chilly bus, and hauled my bruised hopes home.

***

As a child I used to puzzle over the story of Adam and Eve and the Garden of Eden, which, according to the paintings in my *Children's Bible*, was like a sunnier version of my grandparent's green and blossoming garden in Oxford. I was perplexed, not by the similarities with its stream and overhanging willow tree, nor by the boughs laden with apples, but by the fact that apparently nobody had ever tried to find it. I mean, I was OK, for the time being I had trips to Granny and Granddad, but not everyone did. Why, I wondered, did nobody search out that Middle Eastern paradise so distinctly located by the rivers running from it and the fiery sword-wielding man-beast on the front gate? It had to be hard to miss, even if you weren't looking for it. What was the likelihood of people going about their hot and dusty journeys through the belly of Babylonia and not one day coming across an overgrown enclave of lush blooming vegetation? And, in their excited search for the way in, what were the chances of them not discovering a path, at the end of which flames a sword in the clutch of a roaring cherubim? That would be news, right? But there's been no word. No photographs of Indiana Jones-type heroes wrangling with the angelic bouncer on the door or, better still, bypassing the angel and parachuting in at last to the bliss of the Lost Paradise of Eden. As my mother shook her head at my persistent questions, I kept puzzling over and over in my mind. Surely somebody's found a way back.

It took a few years for me to realize that the Eden of my Bible picture books was not the kind of sprawling oasis of roses and apple trees I could expect to find along the grid references of a map. That it doesn't exist like some kind of free love commune nestled at the mouth of the Tigris and Euphrates. That its truth doesn't lie in proof that Adam and Eve were actual people living in an actual garden called Eden. It took a while for me to realize that the truth of this paradise with all its love, nakedness and fearlessness resonates much deeper into the human spirit than creationist propaganda ever will. Because, beyond stories about apples and fig-leaf bikinis, it becomes our story too: the story that we are trying to live here in the twenty-first century. It reminds us what human beings are created to be – unafraid and connected, whole and exhilarated by generosity. It's a picture of what relationship can be when you're at home in your own skin, at ease with yourself, not cringing in shame or wizened by jealousy and resentment. The story of Eve and Adam's nakedness speaks of peace within themselves and with each other.

As far as our lives go, it isn't a state we enjoy most of the time. I am not always at one with those around me. My attempts to be the consistently loving wife, mother, daughter, sister, friend, and priest that I want to be are continually flummoxed, and mostly I'm too attuned to the sating of my own needs and surmounting my own fears to be present to those I encounter. All isn't well. And how I know it isn't well is because somewhere in me is a memory of Eden. There are moments of recollection when I connect with others and the fragmented parts of myself come together for a while and echo a memory that tells me I'm Home. It's a sort of ancient remembering in the soul that reminds me that all the pocks of fear and inadequacies gashed across my life are exactly that – blights and sabotage that I recognize and can name because deep down I know it wasn't meant to be like this.

How else could suffering be named if we had no blueprint for peace and truth? I remember it.

You have moments of remembering it.

And Eve and Adam remembered it too as they experienced for the first time the cold hostility and curdling shame of their nakedness before each other and their God.

For a while it had all been good and Adam and Eve had been gloriously happy reflecting the image of the Creator. But then came the moment when the serpent offered them another possibility: why settle for that when you could *be* the Creator? Why stand under the waterfall when you could harness the power of the entire river? And so, reaching to grasp control, they bite into the fruit that promises to make them like God. They lose their place and they lose their bearings.

Imagine it: all you have ever been is breathed into being by Love, fully seen and fully known and fully delighted in. Imagine how it would be to realize, too late, the devastating mistake of stepping out of that flow and seeing yourself for the first time without Love. Recoiling with dismay, you see what you are reduced to without Love's life-giving gaze.

The ruptures don't stop there though, they crack on rumbling beyond your naked bewilderment, and you look across and see your beloved now strange and altered. You look into their eyes but all you see is judgement. The space between you, which you had shared and explored and in which you had made love, is now warped. And then you realize that they too now see you differently, that without the cover of Love they will look into your eyes and be reminded of their shame.

This is how the story goes and this is how the story still goes, because it turns out that we are a lot like them. We are like the woman and the man in that poem; uneasy with ourselves, often unreachable to each other and striving relentlessly to find our way Home. We are like them in the way we hear accusation bellowing through the undercurrents of our many interactions. In the way that fear suffocates the hope from our desires. In the way our inadequacy tempts us to blame something or, usually, someone else. We share with them our unease at the thought of not finding a place to belong, or thinking we have nothing to offer to the flourishing of the world.

In the wrestle with fear, shame and blame, Eve lives on, because it turns out that I am a lot like Eve. I too have reached for the cover of leaves that are close to hand. I have spent my energy gathering them, arranging them into the kind of protection that a girl looks for in this exile from Eden. Like Eve, I can't bear all that has gone wrong and no longer fits, especially when it's me that is wrong and doesn't fit. Like Eve, with her decorative attempt to cover shame and mistakes, I have tried to put my world right, tried to cover the gaps and gloss over my faults.

The truth is that I have tried to find a way back to Eden. We all have in our brave and deluded way. Wearing many different leafy disguises I have tried to claw and clamber my way back, believing that somehow, if I could just be good enough, I would make it. This is a story about those torn leaves and what they have now become as they lie mulching into compost beneath my feet. This is the story of how my own efforts to control and uphold the images I wanted to believe about myself tripped me up. And it is a rediscovery of a small, often overlooked line in that poem: that after we fall and lose our leaves there is something else; there is Love.

'And so God made tunics of skins for the man and his wife and clothed them.'

But first they had to lose the leaves.

1

The Insiders

There was a time when I thought that in order to be a real Christian you had to have had a bad start in life. It seemed that people who got up to tell their stories at church or at youth rallies or summer camp had always had a rocky childhood, probably taking up a spot on the social services' At Risk register, before degenerating into the dark world of drugs and crime where, as a gang member, they were on the verge of an early death when a Christian turned up and shared God's love with them. After going cold-turkey and being born again, these former addicts turned their lives around for God, left their gangs and became youth workers or travelling evangelists, sharing their exciting conversion stories with impressionable young people like me.

In actual fact I probably wasn't exposed to very many people like this. The likelihood is that the two most gripping contemporary Christian stories in the 1980s were repeated so often that they became conflated in my mind. One was about a violent New York gang leader's conversion, the other about a young woman missionary from England helping members of the Hong Kong triad gangs to get off heroin through prayer. The take-home message was kind of confusing. Since gang warfare was not a feature of life on the streets of Cheltenham we guessed this meant we were being ushered towards a life on the mission field, making up for the lack of grave sin in our pre-Jesus lives by reaching out to those unfortunates who had it in spades.

Together with a few other couples, my parents had started up a church congregation in one of the grittier neighbourhoods of our town which, when you discover the leafy and affluent place that is Cheltenham Spa, cannot lay claim to the desolations of a true inner-city urban priority area. Nevertheless church families moved into the area, and around the corner from our house stood our little meeting hall with its sign outside: Emmanuel Church – God is with us. That's what we were about: showing that God was here among these streets where children roamed, instructed by parents not to come home until 10 p.m., where cars sat burnt out, having sated for a little while the boredom of kids looking for a thrill. Here we were hoping to make good on the sign outside our church, showing that God definitely was here for the woman heartbroken by her husband now in prison for abusing their children; for the children in Sunday school whose parents had died of alcoholism and cancer and who were about to be taken into care; and for the mentally ill woman who would call our house and leave menacing messages, provoking a spate of nightmares after I once inadvertently answered the phone to her. Referred to by Mum and Dad as an "open home", our house was a place of rest and kindness and listening for anyone troubled or in difficulty.

So we saw such troubles because our church was a place where people were welcomed with all their messiness and loneliness. From our little corrugated-roofed hall on this council estate the church family absorbed those who were shaken, broken, tired or hopeless. And to us children church was just a group of families and grownups who were good and wise and kind and stable; people who mopped up the problems instead of creating them.

These situations being discussed, these strange people sitting at our dinner table, the man for whom Mum was making up the camp bed in the sitting room while Dad made coffee to sober him up, they all appeared with regularity in our home but they remained Other. There was us and there was them. We were born into this goodness and belonged to it, we kids were on the inside and could only see the needy and the tormented as outsiders finding their way Home. The only time it became a disappointment was when Outsiders got up to tell their story about how God had saved them from drugs and self-destruction. We couldn't compete with that kind of repentance.

***

I had a conversation with a priest once about Adam and Eve and what they were really trying to get when they decided to take a bite of the forbidden fruit. Because, seriously, why? What did they want that they didn't have already? The priest suggested that they wanted power, they desired the kind of knowledge that would give them greater power.

But I wonder if it really was that, because that sounds like a post-Eden response. That's the sort of thing we do now because we are trying to feel better about not being in Eden. But back then, when Eve took the fruit, all she knew, lived and breathed was beauty and harmony. She didn't need power because there were no chore wars, no surreptitious point-scoring, no clocking up how often she was the first to apologize. Just a blissful mutuality that the rest of us can only try to imagine.

None of the games, the fear, or manipulation: just enjoyment in each other.

In that kind of idyll of peace and love what need would you have for power? When you are an insider, your face reflecting the glory of God and your name spoken into being by that same Creator. When you are whole and known – why do you need to grab power?

When your heart is uncluttered by regrets because you've never acted out of deceit or withheld yourself out of fear or laziness … When your future is unclouded by doubts because you've not learned to be afraid, why do you need strong defences? When nothing drains the life from you or makes you feel distant and disconnected from your beloved, why would it even cross your mind to look for something else to bolster your sense of self?

Of course, you don't see that you were never meant to be the Source of Life. You don't yet know, as you reach for that fruit, that once your eyes are opened and you see the choice between good and bad, you won't have the strength always to choose the good. That integrity and completeness will be eroded by the constant possibility of choosing things that will please you alone; things that will divide you from your partner and undo the harmony of your life together. You can't yet know that the knowledge of good and evil will inevitably lead to death because you will choose ways that do not bring life.

And so it is only as you step onto that pedestal in imitation of God that the ground beneath you begins to give way and you realize you're no longer secure. That now you are fractured, exposed and lost in a garden that was once yours and now no longer feels like home. You feel unable to navigate a way through the possibilities and opportunities and desires rushing at you.

You thought that the fruit of this tree would bear you up, fuelling you as you took your godlike place over everything. But now you look at yourself with a different kind of sight. Now you see yourself outside of the knowing love with which God had always covered you. The garden that you had grown and tended, and over which you thought you could reign, is now just a good hiding-place to buy you some time till you figure out how to feel like an insider once again.

2

Baptism

The little mission church that we had moved to set up stood a few hundred yards from our house. It was a 30-second walk but that stroll each Sunday morning carried with it the purpose and vision of the mission field all the same. Before we were born, Mum had lived in Africa working alongside a nun and a Dutch monk, Brother Tarcisius, caring for polio victims across Ghana. Together they worked with a multitude of children whose limbs were missing; rehabilitating them, teaching them to walk and study and doing what they could to throw off the superstition that disability is a curse from the gods.

Dad had also been working in Africa, at an outpost called Gulu in Uganda, just as Idi Amin was making his bid for power. Dad stayed there, dispensing his medicines in some backwater hospital, dodging a misplaced attempt on his life, before returning to England and training to be a teacher. But the heartbeat of his faith never dwindled in its missionary vision.

Returning from Africa, both of them chose to settle in the south west of England and, at a Christmas party of mutual friends, this tall beauty in a floor-length blue dress captured Dad's eye, and apparently also the gaze of every other man present. She, having recently featured in the pages of *Tatler* Magazine, looked every bit as unreachable as women like that seem to be – until he heard her speaking about life working with Voluntary Services Overseas in Africa. Their friendship crossed the breadth of class division and the two of them discovered love, faith and a mutual desire to live life's adventures to the full.

Of course, we all have our own idea of how those visions will look. And when they actually unfold they tend not to be the picture we dreamed up. So I am sure that, when they began talking about the far-off places in the world to which they could go and make a contribution, they had no clue that the exciting pull of non-government organizations (NGO) job opportunities would give way to the needs of their own son and his particular disabilities.

I was the eldest child; four years later my sister, Rosalind, arrived. Between us was Alastair, the crumpled, five-pound bundle that my father held in the palm of his hand, before the doctors realized something was wrong and rushed him away for tests. I was too young to remember it but along the way I absorbed the two stories my parents tell of that time. Mum, lying in her hospital bed with an inexplicable lack of feeling or love for the baby she'd just born, until the doctors brought Alastair back to her along with the news that they had diagnosed Down's syndrome, at which point she reached for this tiny baby and love came rushing in.

Dad's story is of the following Sunday at church, where he was playing the organ, with me standing knee-high next to him, while the tears streamed down his face as he began to take in this news and the new future that this child would bring. After the service was over and the news had been announced to the rest of the congregation, Dad found himself being the one to comfort shocked friends who gathered around him. The friendship and support offered by this congregation meant that church was not so much a building but our wider family.

When Mum became pregnant again the medical monitoring kicked in much earlier, a close eye being kept on both baby and mother. When this little one threatened to make a dangerously early entry into the world Mum was prescribed an old-fashioned confinement and spent several months in hospital. It was during this time that doctors suspected the baby had spina bifida and, given the family situation (which was a delicate way of referring to Alastair), pressed Mum to consider further tests.

And, once they had drawn long breaths, Mum and Dad did just that. They chose to consider the future and this child and, once again letting go of their imagined plans, chose to see the future together as a gift. Whoever this baby was it would be a gift to them and, ruling out more tests, they prepared to welcome it and be the family it would need.

I have a scar on my leg where I fell off a swing at a party one August day when I was four. I can still remember that tumble, the gash on my thigh, and the bloody mess on my party dress. I remember wanting my Mum and searching for her through all the grown-ups who seemed to be running to pick me up. But Mum was in a bloody mess all of her own back at the hospital, where my sister was making her way into the world. Rosalind arrived plump, hungry and prepared to shout about it. The anxieties that had hung over her existence all the months she had been growing, unknown in the womb, dissipated: there was no evidence of spina bifida nor any other disability.

And so we were three. Three Jepson children welcomed into the warm embrace of two go-getter parents who had once had plans to live far away and make their small change for good in the world. In the cocoon of the Emmanuel Church family we grew and listened and duly took on the assurances that there was an even bigger love than that of our parents. We added our little voices to the song, making our theological assent that, "Jesus loves us this we know, for the Bible tells us so".

We listened to the story of Jesus' baptism in a river and how the skies were torn open and a dove descended upon him while a voice was heard from the heavens declaring that Jesus was God's beloved and pleasing son. We listened to the story and imagined what it looked like to see the skies ripped apart and wondered whether you could see God's face as he held the clouds back and boomed his affirmation and love. We looked at the photos of our baptisms and saw the water dripping off our tiny heads, and we listened as we were told that we too are loved by God and called His children. I nodded and wondered why the church roof was not ripped in two where God was supposed to have leaned in to make His baptismal declaration of love and delight over us.

We accepted the news that we were loved ultimately by God, but there was no way to compute how it could be bigger than Mum and Dad's because there was just love.

Until, each in our own time, we discovered there wasn't.

There wasn't just love, there was judgement and, as we walked home from school one day, there was the cruelty of a boy whose face contorted and mouth opened, hurling its disgust upon Alastair, the spit shattering on the pavement as it landed by his feet.

Feeling sick and furious I walked Ali home and recounted what had happened to Mum who listened quietly, all the time making our afternoon snack, as if she'd been preparing for this conversation for a long time. Without any grief or indignation she calmly explained that Alastair would get reactions like this from people; that, despite my incredulity, other people would fear him because he's different. The only indication for this so far was that he went to a different school from Rosalind and me. And so she patiently explained that his face, his features, those tiny ears and eyes uplifted at the corners would provoke name-calling, taunts and teasing from people who didn't know how to respond to him in any other way.

I don't realize yet that the sound of God's love breaking through the skies and the holy water running over his brow like the tender touch of a father's hand will be drowned out by the burden of labels like "Down syndrome" and "mongoloid" and "handicapped".

And so we begin our exile from the Eden of our parents' unconditional love, ushered out by the sounds of unheavenly judgements. It will be years before we rediscover those words spoken over Jesus at his baptism and come to realize once more that they are for us too, and that they cannot be unsaid by any accusations or embellished by our attempts to be good.

3

Exile

The cataclysmic fall-out from those nibbles of the forbidden fruit, the realization that we are naked and exiled from the Garden, sends tremors through every aspect of our life, from uncomprehending spouses to fear about the future, from Seasonal Affective Disorder to a disappointing glance in the mirror. It assaults us in whopping collisions of our will with that of another's; it drenches us in downpours of disappointment from which we find no cover; or disorients us with the news that we are not as safe in life as we first thought we were. It announces itself in the spit of an angry boy who needs to launch his misplaced disgust upon a child with differently slanted features. And I remember when news of my own exile was delivered to me in a very particular way.

It was our final term at junior school when Rachel Humsley, a girl in my class, approached my desk and leaned in to enquire whether I was going to have braces. I'd assumed everyone had braces. As far as I knew it was a rite of passage once you reached secondary school. We all read books where teenagers have braces and hate it, and we figured out that those characters were created to make all of those real teenagers with a mouthful of metal feel less sad and lonely. So yes, I suppose I would have braces.

"Because you would be pretty if it wasn't for your teeth."

This was disquieting news. Like I had just been entered into a category of a contest I hadn't realized I was meant to be practising for. I hadn't realized that being pretty was something that would have to matter to me. But now I was being told, matter of factly and without spite, that I was in the race and I wondered what this would mean for me. Within months I discovered.

Foddered into an enormous local secondary school at the age of eleven, I was exposed to the judgement of every scornful boy and girl I was unlucky enough to be noticed by. This was no longer primary school where we no longer noticed what each other looked like because we had grown into comfortable familiarity. The recognition that, on the cusp of an adolescent growth spurt, my teeth were beginning to jut out of my mouth at odd angles had passed most of my classmates by. But Rachel Humsley, a latecomer to Christchurch Primary, was a portent of the ridicule I was about to experience among 1,500 teenagers.

On a bright morning in early September Julia, a girl from church, called for me and, scooting my bike out of the garage, we set out for the first time on our journey to a new school, crisp in our brand new navy and emerald uniforms.

In the reception area large signs were placed directing Year 7 down the ramp towards the hall. Beyond the doors the drone of 220 nervous boisterous pupils rumbled as they buzzed around looking for their old friends, plucked up courage to begin making new ones and tried to find others with the same colour button on their jumper. I was in Curie, which was yellow, but in the confusion of brown, green, blue, purple and red buttons darting around me I made my way to the edge of the hall and began circling it looking for the twins, Louise and Jess, girls who were also in Curie. I found them standing near a smart, bespectacled man who looked like a wrinkly hound-dog, and was relieved to discover that this was Mr Williams, our new housemaster.

Class 7C, as we were about to become, followed Mr Williams back up the ramp into reception and on through a maze of corridors towards a spacious wing of the school. Scanning the faces of the other boys and girls for friendly smiles I waited to be assigned to a seat. And so my mind was elsewhere when, as I took my desk next to an unknown boy, I heard someone behind me comment that it was too bad he'd got "Goofy". That was the first name I heard and I didn't even realize it was referring to me. Turning to the boy next to me I shyly introduced myself, "Hi, I'm Joanna."

His body turned towards me, one arm resting on his new desk and the other along the back of his chair, and a kind of amusement on his face. I waited expectantly for this friendly boy to tell me his name.

Instead he turned and guffawed to the boy behind.

"Oh my god, you're right!"

"I've never seen teeth like that for real."

"I am actually sitting by the living, breathing Goofy."

This time I heard it, but still its cultural reference was almost lost on me; I'd never seen the Disney film and was only vaguely aware that one of Goofy's characteristics were two teeth poised like overhanging tombstones from below his protruding snout. So I wasn't hurt by the name-calling, only by the unseen barrier that had mysteriously prevented me from making friends with the boy I would have to sit beside for the next year. I didn't get the joke that he was making with the kid behind us but I didn't need to get it. Turning back to the front I sat silently, doodling on the inside of my fresh exercise book, wishing I could have been paired with one of the twins, or even Andrew Wells, the nerdiest boy in Sunday school.

I had been trying to keep a grip on today, trying to find the stepping stones of familiarity to get me across the maelstrom of strangeness and overwhelming enormity of this new life in senior school, I was trying to reach out and build bridges. Now here I was, somehow blind to a fault of which I hadn't been aware but knew that I needed to figure out fast. Then we could sit together and get on and talk, like equal human beings.

That evening over supper Mum and Dad were keen to hear how my first day had gone, and so I pieced together my day for them with descriptions of teachers who seemed nice and friends with whom I'd been reunited. Dutifully I got out my timetable for Dad to inspect, his eagerness that my science and maths would now improve tempered by the limited appearances they made on my schedule of classes. As soon as I had finished helping to clear away supper, I escaped up to my room and looked up the word "goofy" in my encyclopedia.

* * *

A few months before starting senior school I had performed in a show produced by my dance school and my class had been given the lamentable role of portraying a shadowy underwater blob. No girl goes into ballet to play the part of a blob, underwater or not. Girls start doing ballet because they want to be transformed by tutus and satin and sequins into something breathtaking and marvellous. And to have the chance, in a Darcey Bussell kind of way, to get on stage and show everyone how breathtaking and marvellous they are.

After the final performance of "The Snow Bird", which unaccountably featured this underwater blob, a trail of disappointed and frustrated ten-year-olds exited the stage door of the theatre wondering how to put into words their existential angst at being relegated to this useless and ugly part. We'd wanted to be snowbirds in white sparkly tutus and feathers, daintily flitting across the stage and delighting the audience with our effortless *grands jetés*. Instead we were clad in black catsuits with face-paint and lipstick to match and bits of torn bin-liners billowing out behind us. Later on Mum had commented on how well I danced my part, to which I retorted, "How did you know? It's not like you could distinguish one part of the blob from another." And without malice came the answer, "We could tell it was you from your teeth." In a nebulous body of blackened dancers it seems I could stand out from the crowd, the whites of my pointy front teeth breaking through the black-lipped anonymity of the rest of the dancers. So somewhere in my mind was an awareness that my teeth were noticeable to others and that the name "Goofy" was probably referring to them. But only now did it become a taunt, an accusation: an identity. My mouth began to feel like a mask from which I couldn't step out; leaving a shadow of Joanna invisible behind the barrage of names hammered onto me.

Maybe if you're eleven when you start hearing these things about yourself you're too young to get defensive. Maybe you have to know that there is something to defend in the first place. Maybe if I had been eleven and thought I was destined to be a super-model then I would have got agitated and upset at being told my limb-to-height ratio was just nowhere near long enough for that career path. But those kind of life-expectations and values were not on the radar of eleven-year-old me. Sure, I'd had Barbies but I had never expected to one day *be* Barbie. I liked being a Brownie, and going on summer camp, and roller-skating parties, and watching Davy Jones in The Monkees. I loved ballet, and had read in a book that ballet dancers had to be tall but not too tall and have pretty hands. Pretty hands, I pondered. And I looked to see whether my hands had the potential to reach the required level of prettiness.

I also loved Anne of Green Gables and she was taunted at school. She got called "Carrots" because of her red hair. Perhaps that was why I loved Anne and looked up to her, because she had the guts to break a slate over the bully's head. But when, during the Christmas of 1987, the film appeared on television it turned out that Anne was a beautiful redhead. So smart and alabaster-browed that Gilbert Blythe only teased her because he was in love with her. I looked in the mirror to see if that could be the case for me too. But my hair was brown and I was in bottom set for maths. Nobody was mistaking their love for derision in my case.

When sent to get something from the school librarian one afternoon I was bewildered to realize that I had become a muse for the jibes of a table full of boys. Pretending to stifle their laughter they attempted, in stage whispers, to outwit each other with comedy descriptions of my jaws. They were Year 11 boys. I should have been invisible to them. And in a way I was. I was not Joanna: I was chipmunk, can-opener, wood-chipper, metal-masher, scrap car-crusher. All of which might be very cool things to identify with – if you're a boy combining imagined superpower abilities with your love of all things big and mechanical. But for this eleven-year-old girl it did not signal a hidden superhero alter ego. The daily round of names came like incantations, banishing me to the edges where I must watch without a voice or part to play. The Chosen were gathered up into experiments with make-up, and gossip about boys and party invitations. The Unchosen were condemned to look in from the outside where our buck teeth or ginger hair or thick NHS glasses or dumpy thighs had relegated us, stunted and silent.

In the Easter holidays, when I asked the hairdresser to cut my hair into a bob the way other girls were styling theirs, I didn't see what a mistake it would be. Returning to school on Monday the class bully, and my personal nemesis, Tessa Drew, a deep-voiced drama queen for whom the boundary between imagination and real life were so blurred she was openly known as a pathological liar, stood up to answer the tutor as to why she was laughing during registration. "Jo's face, Sir. From the side it looks like her teeth have munched a straight line through her hair."

Pausing for an eruption into husky laughter she made way for the class to turn and look at me, before continuing to play to the class-wide audience she had now drawn in.

"I was just saying that it's a shame her teeth can only cut a line at that one length. Now you can see that she's got no chin."

This time it seemed Tessa was at least attempting to tell the truth. As Mr Perrott's bemused gaze followed the laughter across the classroom to where I sat, I quietly pressed my chin and mouth into my hands, and vowed never to cut my hair short again. It turns out that after a while outside the warmth of Eden the cold does get to you. You realize you are exposed and in need of something to shield and comfort you.

It's funny, isn't it, that when Adam and Eve took their bites of the forbidden fruit they knew that they were naked? They knew that everything was different now, that their sense of belonging was ruined and replaced by the need to hide. It wasn't God who came along and told them to run and hide. They saw it themselves; it was their own judgement on each other that declared them shameful and in need of some foliage to hide behind. God never said, "Good grief, look at yourselves! You're naked! You ought to be ashamed of yourselves ... you'd better string some leaves together and hide." We hear that from other voices.

4

Angels and Demons

Over long months my hair slowly grew long enough for me to brush it down to hide the worsening protrusion of my growing face. No longer just a case of goofy gawkiness, my adolescent bones now developed so that my upper jaw pushed forward exposing my teeth, pointed like the bow of a ship. Perhaps if my lower jaw had also grown forward to match it I could have justified the nickname "metal-crusher", but instead it failed to grow much at all and, with the lack of a clearly defined chin, my face seemed to disappear down into my long neck. The arrangement of this rather wonky facial architecture made it impossible to hold my lips closed together, though in moments where I thought there was dignity to be salvaged I would brave the discomfort. Like when I met someone new and wanted to hold out as just a regular-faced-girl, before being outed as *NFWK*.

With new people there's a chance. How long do they say you've got? Thirty seconds? Seven seconds? One tenth of a second to get that person to see you and like you and believe that there is something worth knowing? I could keep my lips shut together for less than ten seconds, which meant my bids for a new friendship might just succeed, if it weren't for the crooked shape made while smiling with my mouth shut. Sooner or later the hope of meeting and making a new friend would collapse in the taut grimace of my pursed smile, or with the gush of words revealing not just my name but an unexpected flash of pink, bony jaw.

If I'd lived in a world where faces were not the litmus test against which a person was judged or if I had simply learned not to take to heart the judgement of my peers then I would have continued, as I had since I was a child, to smile uncompromisingly. In the face of new friendship I would have smiled widely and openly, allowing the edges of my eyes to crinkle with mischief and glee. That is the story I would like to have written – about how, at twelve years old, I faced my tormentors and frenemies with an unshaken belief in who I was. How I met the stares of school peers with unblinking self-possession, rooted in the knowledge of all that I knew lay behind that misshapen fraction of my face. But at twelve years old I wasn't telling the world who I was, because I was listening to voices that were giving me the answer: the wrong voices – the ones that summed all of me up as defective and ugly. Voices that dismissed the whole of me in a scourge of name-calling about my mouth.

When girls giggled about a boy they fancied and dreamily etched his name inside their pencil-case, I looked on not daring to mention the boy I had spied in Year 10 whom I would watch playing football at lunchtime. It was not my place to have crushes. If I had named a crush out loud my friends would have to acknowledge him and cheer me on in this new drama. They would have to sound like they believed something could happen between him and me. It would be like standing on the sidelines of a hockey game talking animatedly about the goal you were hoping to score. I couldn't bear provoking the look of embarrassment in their eyes while they searched around for some disingenuous words of encouragement.

It's not that you forget the other voices, the voices of love that tell you who you are and where you have come from; it's just that you allow other voices to grow louder. You give them more airtime, listening and learning that not all of you is acceptable or welcomed. And so you begin cordoning off parts of yourself, silencing them and shunning them. Until you are fractured and unwhole, unable to look at what doesn't seem to fit, or to embrace all the unfinished parts of yourself and no longer sure how to let the beautiful or the broken parts reflect the light.

There were moments of mercy when I was caught in the light of another's reach. Strange occurrences where, through the crush of bodies heaving along the one-way corridor at break time, I was seen, not as sport to trample against the wall, but as something else. I don't really know what, because what could account for a Year 10 girl reaching through the door and pulling me out of the throng and into the safety of her classroom? Popular, talented and distinctively impish Beckie Harper was one half of the identical Harper twins, recognizable to anyone in a crowd from their eruptions of pale fluffy hair. Three years above me, the twins were the kind of girls I knew but who certainly wouldn't know me. So I'm not convinced that Beckie really recognized me from way back in junior school when she hauled me in and offered me a table to sit on while I ate my crisps. She was just very kind. Which is how I became friends with Beckie and her friend Lauren, and began a rhythm of lunchtime escapes from school, accompanying them on walks across the fields and scrambling through hedges to the forbidden woods beyond. With them there was never any need to explain the misery that school had become; I guessed that they already knew that and that's why I was here with them, invited to tag along.

When, one day, after a group of girls rounded on me in the girls' loos stabbing their fingers at my torso and shouting that I was the cause of all ugliness in Curie house, Beckie and Lauren listened with serious faces, unfazed by what they were hearing. Kindness shone, not in phony attempts to tell me I was fine or in pretence that my face wasn't really problematic for other kids, but in their determination to open up a different vista for me. They asked questions about what I liked, what was I good at, who my friends were, and trod carefully to find out if life was any easier outside the school campus. Discovering that church was the main feature of life beyond school, Beckie invited me to her confirmation service at Christchurch. When I told them I loved dancing she found out where my ballet school was and turned up with Emma the following Saturday to see if I was free to wander into town with them after my class. But it was too late. The lazy Saturday pastime of wandering around town had begun to induce cramps of fear, causing my stomach to revolve turbulently. Going to town was about buying stuff: clothes, make-up, things that would make you look better. It was about seeing people, and I no longer wanted to be seen or reminded that I didn't fit, and that no amount of make-up or new clothes could alter that.

Saturday was where I reclaimed territory and made the world my own again. It was spent in ballet lessons, and cycling over to Jane's where we rearranged her parent's basement into an office suite in which we played out our business idea. "Problem Page" was a couple of desks, two telephones, a pile of notepads for our case files and us, with our fake American accents. We had to have accents and they had to be American – it added instant sophistication to what was otherwise a game of social workers answering the phone on imagined basket-cases and proceeding to solve their problems. It could have all run its course within the space of a couple of Saturdays, except it ran on for months once we introduced the added plot-line of our imaginary boyfriends, Dan and

Tim. Interspersing our client calls every once in a while we would lean back on our swivel chairs and, thinking ourselves into the heavyheartedness of a woman in love, solemnly tell each other the difficulties of our love lives. All with very bad American accents.

Problem Page was my turf; an afternoon a week where I could put things right and life's impossibilities could be waved away by my soothing, simple answers. Here I knew what I was about, because in this bunker no other voice but mine could be heard. The imaginary clients unloading their imaginary woes were my chance to be something; they asked me for help and gave me a voice that I hadn't worked out how to use anywhere else. Into the receiver of that old disconnected phone I seized the opportunity to speak words that proved that I was not my teeth, my braces, a girl hiding behind her hair. I was grown up, independent, useful and had my stuff together.

5

Good News Crusaders

Then once a year, another spacious place appeared on the landscape of my summer as our family packed up the caravan to head 20 miles down the road to the Malvern Hills. Specifically the Three Counties Showground, which for one week a year became home to Good News Crusade Bible camp. We had been attending this annually since I was five, along with most of our church congregation, and the Jepsons were stalwarts; part of the Good News Crusade scene. Mum and Dad were camp counsellors and everyone knew Alastair from his appearances on main stage with his junior-sized guitar accompanying the band.

As a family we were definitely part of the Church of England but for this week in the year you might doubt it. If you had peeked into the Severn Barn where the evening meetings took place you wouldn't have recognized us as a church at all. Under the bright warmth of industrial lights, you would have seen a throng of three, maybe four thousand people dancing up and down between the rows of plastic chairs, faces upturned, eyes closed as a band led them through chorus after chorus of songs. And, as the sound of thousands of voices Lifting the Name of Jesus chorused through the air, you would have seen many arms lifted high too, hands outspread, holding up the words so that God might be assured of this devotion.

You would have felt how the music enveloped us, its joyful melodies shutting out all else, as it erupted across the twilight. Swelling throughout the lower slopes of the Malvern Hills, the rhythm of its muffled beat knocking like the presence of an unwanted visitor on the homes of residents nearby. Then, later, you would have watched us go back to our circles of tents and gather round the huge thermos of hot chocolate where we would pray under the night sky that our praises would win the hearts of those who'd heard us, for Jesus.

Good News Crusade was not church but if it had been I would have been there every day. It was a week of full-on preaching, teaching, praise, worship and fellowship, which was church-speak for hanging out with your pals sharing stories about how good God is. In the afternoons there was a lot of fellowship as people gathered their camping chairs around the space in front of our open caravan awning. Tea was brewed, guitars lazily strummed, children crawled around begging grown-ups for a game of swingball and thoughts on the previous evening's talk were shared. These pow-wows often led to a time of prayer as people testified to how their lives had been changed by what God was doing. This was really what they all came to camp for: to do business with God. The songs, the sermons, the altar calls, the hot chocolate and fellowship were all about encouraging each other to tune in and listen up and get down to soul business. What that business might be depended on where you were with the Lord.

As a child it turns out that there isn't much business to be done with God beyond committing your life to him. So at the age of five, in Glories, the children's meeting, I had repeated the words of the prayer and had taken my first step towards business with God.

"Dear Jesus, I know that you love me. Thank you that you died on the cross to save me. I'm sorry for the things I've done wrong and I ask you to forgive me and come and live in my heart forever. Amen."

My mum wrote the date in the front of my Bible and later on, in years to come, I would almost feel her ticked-box relief as she documented this score. One child saved, two to go. And I was saved. I grew up bilingual, fluent in the religious jargon of these spirit-filled Christians who saw themselves as living water to be poured over the dry, intellectual liberalism that they said the Church of England had become. I grew up knowing that we were Real Christians, not mere churchgoers concerned with superficial stuff like priestly robes and incense.

But it wasn't this that I'd been saved from. It was the social desolation of the other 51 weeks of the year where my face curbed inclusion in the crowd and my parents' rules curbed exposure to sin.

The pursuit of holiness cultivates a kind of loneliness that leaves you, to the relief of anxious Christian parents, running for the safety of other Christian kids. So that week at camp saves me from social death because in that one week I remember that I'm not alone. I find friends who also know what it feels like to be not invited to a movie-sleepover because we won't be allowed to watch the 15 certificate film, and whose classmates soon learn that Sunday is a Family Day so we won't be allowed to go over and hang out and watch TV. At camp I expand into the spaciousness of a place where I belong and am known, a place that operates on a system of belonging that I can navigate.

My friends here completely get it when I tell them how Rosalind and I were banned from attending a visiting theatre company's play at the end of term because it featured a wizard. We sprawl on the grass and they laugh as I describe with despair how my sister and I sat in an empty classroom doing extra maths, along with an excluded boy who was withdrawn from the show as a punishment. This is what it means to be set apart for Jesus: sometimes it feels like a punishment.

That's what Peter Cabot, the children's pastor, tells us in our morning meetings when he talks to us about Jesus' warning that the world will persecute us and hate us because we follow him. And though the narrow path eventually leads to life in all its fullness it seems that the path itself is pretty lonely and hateful. But at least it's wide enough to accommodate my gang of friends: Charlie Fox and his sister Katie, and Hannah, Julia and Joel.

If Harry Potter had been published whilst I was a child I would have begged to be home-schooled: a playground full of Hogwarts chatter and fantasy quidditch would have been unbearable. Wizardry and witchcraft were up there with horoscopes and crystals in occult dabbling that was forbidden to us – except, that is, when we got hold of the autobiography of a former witch, telling the story of her conversion to Christianity. None of our parents worried when we got hold of *From Witchcraft to Christ* from the camp bookshop and pored over its details about covens and black magic. When Joel told us that his mum was a friend of the author, we pestered him for details about what she was like: Did she still have the look of a witch about her? Did she still carry the evil scars of this former life? We were captivated, not just because it was sensationalist but because it was sensational and real. There were rumours that covens of witches met in the hills above our campsite and Charlie insisted that he'd tagged along on a midnight walk with some of the youth team where they had stumbled on the burnt remnants of an animal skull. Unequivocal signs of occult activity, we all agreed, shivering in the grip of these spooky tales.

In short, witches who tell their testimony about a pre-Christian life spent stirring cauldrons were fine. Wizards in theatre were a complete no-go. Doing business with God was our main goal, but dealing with pesky Satan on the side was something we couldn't afford to trivialize. We had joined God's holy army and our fight was not against flesh and blood but against the rulers, authorities and powers of spiritual forces in the heavenly realms. Which was why, when my cousin's Hollywood success catapulted her into movie-stardom in *Ghostbusters* and the girls in my class stuck pictures of her inside their exercise books, Rosalind and I were banned from watching her rise to fame as the demon-possessed Dana. Demonic activity was not to be taken lightly and messed around with by Hollywood or anyone else. Sneaking cuttings from magazines into my books, I would read articles and interviews with her and wonder if she had come through the whole film-making process unscathed.

* * *

Then, at the age of twelve, I was accidentally initiated into the realities of such supernatural battles. It was the Thursday afternoon of camp; I was by myself and possibly twitching for something with which to impress Charlie Fox, and so I headed into the Big Top youth meeting. You were meant to be sixteen or over to attend these meetings but I wandered in unchallenged and slipped into a seat at the end of a row.

When we were five, in Glories, the children's activities were all about love and singing songs that reminded us how we have a wonderful friend in Jesus. At eight we joined Salt Pot, and learned that Jesus calls us to be like salt in a world where people don't know him.

At sixteen, in the Youth Tent, the emphasis changed: to sex.

Not having it but saving it – for your future husband or wife.

I probably knew this would be the topic when I meandered into the Big Top, and maybe I was hoping to glean enough juice from this grey-haired preacher man's sex talk to silence Charlie's boasts about his brush with a satanic coven on the hills. But at twelve years old, and in no danger of having sex with anyone, this meeting was way past my pay grade.

As the preacher man began to draw his talk to a close he signalled to the band to play something gently while he invited people to come forward and respond to his altar call. Eyes were closed, praise songs sung, hands opened and people began to wait for the Holy Spirit to prompt them to take the brave steps out of their seat and walk up to the front where someone would be waiting to pray for them.

From behind the strands of hair I had pulled forward to twiddle with, I peeked out at the teenagers beginning, one by one, to get up and make their way to the grassy space near where preacher man was now getting specific.

"And you know that you have strayed from what God wants for your life … you've compromised your relationship with Him, you've given in to lust and sexual temptation …"

I listened up.

The band were still softly strumming.

"You know you need to confess and be made clean; you know God wants to restore you to a right relationship with Him …"

I spied Alice, a girl from church sheepishly making her way towards the gathering crowd beneath the preacher's lectern, her shoulders hunched over in embarrassment.

And then, from somewhere among the bowed teenagers and prayer counsellors, a shriek cut across the preacher man's spiel. In wide-eyed alarm I scrutinized the faces of the band on stage; nobody seemed to show any reaction and yet the lingering cry had definitely come from up at the front somewhere.

Then again, a wail followed by a wild scream, as if someone was watching their friend being stabbed to death before their eyes.

Now I was on my feet. And preacher man was about to jump in too. The scream had come from the crowd; I could see the knot of people shuffle to make a clearing for whoever was in distress, and now preacher man was making his way into the fray. I didn't even realize that the young woman next to me was pregnant when I jumped onto her knee flinging my arms around her neck, sobbing with the terrified realization that this was the sound of a demon being exorcised.

On reflection, maybe if I had seen *Ghostbusters* – *The Exorcist*, even – I would have been much more prepared for the experience and better able to handle it with aplomb. But in my undignified hysteria I remained clinging while the woman and her husband tried to persuade me everything was OK.

It really wasn't OK.

Apart from finding myself in a scene from a horror film, I was about to be spotted by a teenager from church. Hayley hauled me off the pregnant woman and ushered me past the prayer ministry area out of the Big Top. I just glimpsed the writhing girl on the grass before I was led out of a side exit and marched, still sobbing, back to my parents' caravan. I wondered what their take on the situation would be.

Thankfully there was no time of fellowship going on – most folk were trying to round up their children for tea, and Mum was busy making supper inside the caravan. But, once Hayley had explained to Mum what had happened, handing me over to her with the words "I think she's just too young to handle that kind of prayer ministry", Mum decided this was a two-parent situation and sent me off to get Dad from the unit leader's caravan where he was squeezing in the pre-evening prayer meeting with the other counsellors. Now they were actually going to have a situation to counsel.

A caravan with five people in it is a pretty squashed place. A caravan with one child insisting he bring his guitar to the small formica table, an eight-year-old who would rather be eating with her friend in the caravan next door, an inconsolable twelve-year-old and two parents with supper to prepare and a psycho-theological horror scene to assuage is squashed, explosive and messy. I expected, as was usually the case, to be in a whole heap of trouble. I shouldn't have strayed beyond Power Pack. Except that was clearly the least helpful thing to be addressing at this point. They would get to that. In the meantime, baked beans were splashing down Alastair's guitar and Rosalind's friends had come to call for her, and I was declaring I wouldn't be leaving the caravan again for the rest of the week.

So in their wisdom Mum and Dad decided to let the sobs and sniffles subside and the caravan empty of at least some children before reaching for their Bibles and turning to a story in Luke's Gospel.

As Jesus stepped ashore, he was met by a man from the town who had demons in him. For a long time this man had gone without clothes and would not stay at home, but spent his time in the burial caves. When he saw Jesus, he gave a loud cry, threw himself down at his feet and shouted, "Jesus, Son of the Most High God! What do you want with me? I beg you, don't punish me!" He said this because Jesus had ordered the evil spirit to go out of him... Jesus asked him, "What is your name?"

"My name is 'Mob,'" he answered – because many demons had gone into him. The demons begged Jesus not to send them into the abyss.

There was a large herd of pigs near by, feeding on a hillside. So the demons begged Jesus to let them go into the pigs and he let them. They went out of the man into the pigs. The whole herd rushed down the side of the cliff into the lake and drowned."[1]

This story wasn't often used for our Sunday school lessons but I was familiar enough with it to be perplexed by the fate of the pigs. On a purely fiscal level it was pretty unfair on the owner of the herd who lost his livelihood in one dramatic stampede off the side

---

[1] Luke 8.27-33.

of a cliff. And what about the poor pigs themselves, spending their last moments housing a mob of demons before being driven out of control and down to a watery end? And then what did the demons do? Come up for air and start looking for a new repository? It all seemed as if Jesus had gone for rather a short-term solution.

But given the trouble I was in these things seemed like an unnecessary diversion and so I listened quietly to what Dad was saying.

"Darling, I know that what you heard was unpleasant, that it was all very dramatic and startling, but you mustn't focus on that ..."

Mum broke in, "Remember we mustn't give Satan the glory by focusing on the noises and drama."

"But how could I not focus on it? It was terrible ..."

"Then think of that noise as the sound of freedom", Dad offered a little more brightly.

"Think of the release that that girl is going to be feeling now she's been set free and healed ..."

Which was all fine, but the unutterable question going round my mind now was what on earth a teenager could have possibly done to land that kind of demonic force in her life in the first place. And not just any teenager: a teenager who comes to Good News Crusade Bible camp.

I was at camp.

I could be that girl in a few years time.

There was no guarantee that I wouldn't end up demon-possessed if I committed some kind of sin. And I knew I was a sinner. How could I be sure that I wasn't already inflicted with some kind of Satanic presence?

The rush of theological computations left me feeling sick. It also made me change my mind about not leaving the caravan: I needed to stock up on all the prayer and Bible teaching I could get. It would be my insurance against Possession.

Sensing that I might not be taking in any more of their biblical assurances, Dad suggested that we all pray together and then get ready to go to our evening meetings. Bowing our heads, we prayed that Jesus would come and give us peace and renew our trust in his care for us. We prayed for the afflicted girl that she would be free and assured of God's love for her. And we committed ourselves – particularly fervently in my case – to being open to what God wanted to do in our lives for the last two days of camp.

That evening the film being screened for us in the Power Pack tent was *Run Baby Run*, about New York gang leader Nicky Cruz's conversion to Christ. I was perfectly happy to put heavenly warfare right out of my mind and focus back onto the fight against flesh and blood nasties like Nicky Cruz and his homies. And on the back row our little gang chewed on Wham! bars and passed cans of Fanta between ourselves, enjoying the kind of carefree, uncomplicated fellowship that sometimes even kids doing business with God at Bible camp need.

This was the comprehensive schoolgirl who wasn't allowed to watch *Grange Hill* or *Ghostbusters*. The girl who was set apart for Jesus. Set apart from her peers only to be told she is God's light put among them to share with them the Good News.

The good news for me was that once a year I got to be with friends who knew what it was like; who also found salvation in simply belonging.

6

Tongues

Soon we began to observe which preachers guaranteed some demonic action following their altar call. Mostly they were white-haired Americans, but then there was Derek Prince. Dr Prince's prayers were guaranteed to lead to some outburst of dark powers. Charlie loved it and would stand on the concrete ramp leading up to the barn, tucking into his chips, the edges of his mouth vaguely turning up, a studiedly nonchalant observer. I marvelled at the coolness with which he took in what was still a spectacle that surely blew *Ghostbusters* out of the water.

I was neither cool nor amused. I was listening obsessively for the precise wording of Dr Prince's prayer. Because within moments of rounding it up with an, "*In Jesus' name. Amen*", an agonized wail, a dying shriek or desperate roars would be heard from somewhere deep within the rows of people standing waiting. Placing myself close enough to the wide open door not to appear chicken to Charlie, I stood distanced from the blocks of worshippers, maintaining a tight-lipped silence throughout the whole prayer.

The troubling reality was that a startling number of Christians were being exorcised every night. And I couldn't shake the fear that I too might have unwittingly contracted a demon, like a virus that suddenly, unexpectedly, announces its presence with an embarrassing manifestation of symptoms. I wanted to tell someone my fear, but I couldn't in case the demon started kicking off and I had to be carried out by six strong men from the team, foaming at the mouth and roaring with a man's voice like one woman we'd seen. It wasn't much of a choice but I would rather remain ignorantly demonized than go through the public humiliation of descending into excruciating howls. Especially in front of Charlie Fox.

So I worked on my insurance policy. I went to all the meetings, I studied my Bible and lifted up my hands in worship to God, hoping that this would be enough to persuade Him that I really was good, that I was on His side.

When, two years after that first demonic encounter, Peter Cabot invited us to be baptised in the Holy Spirit, I knew this was my moment to notch up some spiritual fortification. I would have the secret language of God: the groans of the Spirit, which St Paul says is God praying within us. Then I would have proof that I really did belong to Christ and wasn't going to end up in hell.

Mum had told me that beginning to pray in tongues felt strange because you have to just open your mouth and start. "It's like learning a new language, with new sounds and noises." And now, here at the front of the Power Pack tent, Peter Cabot told us to do the same. "You've got faith to ask for the Holy Spirit to come and overpower you, now you need to have faith to open your mouth and start speaking in the power of that Spirit."

At school I wasn't very good at languages, but at least there was a textbook answer for how the words ought to sound. Now there was nothing except the hum of children beginning to make their first faltering sounds in the language of God's Spirit and the promise of a more exhilarating fluency than I would ever achieve in French lessons. It wasn't exactly a textbook but the thought of the words my Mum said when praying in tongues was enough to give me something to start with. And so it began: these higgledy-piggledy sounds spilling from my mouth in a language that sounded too odd and disappointing to be the sound of God speaking through me.

It happened to each of us that day. Julia, Charlie, me and Katie pouring out of the Power Pack marquee with everyone else, excited by the buzz of having newly received God's power, laughing about the funny sounds we made, sometimes unsure of whether we had actually prayed in tongues or whether we had slipped into mere imitation of our parents. "I'm sure I was saying 'Shall-I-buy-a-Honda' at one stage", shrieked Julia, recalling the phrase that we had always used when impersonating praying grown-ups at church.

So when, that evening, Hannah found out that we were all changed, filled with the Spirit and spouting tongues in New Testament style, she begged us for a recitation. None of us were prepared to perform for Hannah, Joel and Anthony – the three who had skived off the morning meeting – and their pestering soon gave way to frustrated resentment.

Now there was a divide: those who had and those who had not. Those who spoke in tongues and those who didn't. Perhaps that's where it began to turn sour. Perhaps even in a Bible camp the fear of being left out leaves a kid ready to lash out in any way they can to even the score.

"Go on, just say a few words." Anthony turned to me.

"I'm not going to …"

"Why not?" he persisted.

"It's meant to be prayer, not a performance. Anyway you can hear people speaking in tongues in the meeting tomorrow."

"But I want to hear *you* …"

"Why me?"

He grinned and settled his gaze on my mouth.

"I want to hear if tongues are easier for you to get your teeth around than English."

Katie flushed, her smile at the banter turning to embarrassment at what Anthony was getting at.

This was the kind of moment I needed Charlie's sharp tongue, but he was busy flirting with Hannah.

Only Julia pushed him. "What did you say to her?"

Anthony with his cocky half-smile didn't bother to repeat what he'd said. He just took aim once more.

"I just wondered if her teeth get in the way when she speaks in tongues …" His voice trailed into laughter.

And I began to trail off into the darkness.

Speaking in tongues seemed to have spoiled everything. Three of our gang were left out, and now Anthony had reduced my kindling hopeful prayers to the ugliness of the mouth that tried to utter them. I could speak in tongues but Anthony and his identical twin Joel were dark-eyed boys of epic handsomeness. And now it came down to what mattered more: baptism in the Holy Spirit, or the incontrovertible truth of good looks.

Clearly the Holy Spirit was the one I needed to care about more, the baptism into which I wanted my life to be wholly immersed and transfigured. And yet it wasn't.

Slinking off across the field towards the Severn Barn I thought about praying in tongues right now. Wouldn't this be the moment to pray? With those sighs and groans of the Spirit speaking hopes and longings into life within me? I tried to start; recalling some of the strange phrases my mouth had formed earlier that day. But the sighs of my own spirit were louder and soon hot tears blurred across my eyes and fell onto the grass at my feet. My ambivalence about the Spirit's presence weighed me down in heavy guilt. Despite trying to push away the thought that good looks would have been far better ammunition to deal with life's battles, I knew that it was too late. God knew what I was thinking and I anticipated His displeasure. I couldn't pretend to pray. God was probably regretting wasting this kind of power on such an ungrateful girl. A story surfaced in my mind: the one in Matthew's Gospel where Jesus says to those who claimed they had faithfully followed him, "I never knew you!" I began to picture God booming down at me too, with an exasperated wave of His all-powerful arm, the one He probably used for smiting. "Joanna who? Pah! I never knew you."

But the sound of someone actually calling my name, not in a smitey way, pulled me back from my tearful churning. I recognized the voice, at least, I could narrow it down to one of two people – Anthony or Joel Lowder. While I would never have anticipated Anthony coming to apologize, nor could I have envisaged his twin coming to make amends for his brother's unkindness. And yet, here Joel was, jogging to catch me up and shyly reaching me with the words, "Don't go. Forget what he said."

There was nothing more than that, just his uncomplicated kindness, which, for a moment, rearranged the Laws of Physics. Because someone, to whom the phrase "drop dead gorgeous" evidently belonged, being moved to leave his football alone for a moment and come and find me, defied all I knew about the ways of the world so far.

7

Revival

Feeling powered up and in love with Jesus is easy when you're surrounded by a few thousand other people who have converged for a dedicated week-long love-in with God. It's easy when all your conversations and all the thorny details of life are framed by the bigger picture, a picture of God's love for the world and his plan to make all things new and restored. It isn't just easy to live in that world for a week: it's exhilarating. It's wonderful when every problem isn't just shared but responded to by your fellow Jesus-loving camper with the words "Can I pray with you about that?" When every headache or attitude problem is just another opportunity to experience the power of God's healing in your life. And when every difficult person you encounter is reframed as Satan's attack and evidence that God is doing great things through you.

It's easy to be excited about returning to the real world, ready to see God use you to bring a powerful change in your school, when you're standing among rows of other children all excited about the same thing. When you've been told that your generation are going to be history-makers for Christ and that you're probably not going to die because Jesus is going to return in your lifetime and gather you up in his Rapture, it puts the autumn return to school in a whole new light. It is the mission field to which we are called to be salt and light and to show people the Way. Upon our small shoulders hang school rucksacks and the salvation of our peers. And so every morning and evening I attend the Power Pack meeting with my *Good News Bible*, notebook and pen in hand, ready to receive all the teaching and divine inspiration God wants to impart in preparing me for my return to the mission field of Bournside Comprehensive.

From the front of the marquee shine the words on the overhead projector but we don't need them anymore; they are more than a song now, they have become our hopes and our prayers.

"I am a new creation, no more in condemnation,
Here in the grace of God I stand.
My heart is overflowing, my love just keeps on growing,
Here in the grace of God I stand.
And I will praise you Lord, yes I will praise you Lord,
And I will sing of all that you have done.
A joy that knows no limits, a lightness in my spirit,
Here in the grace of God I stand."

Reaching the crescendo of the chorus repeat once again, Kim, the seventeen-year-old singer, cries out over the music:

"Yes Lord, we want to praise you. We want to sing of all you've done and are doing in our lives. And as we prepare to go back to our homes and our friends and our schools we pray Lord that you would let your kingdom and your power be known through these young people. We pray for each and every one to be filled with your power so that they would become fishers of men, fishers of souls throughout this nation."

Her impassioned prayer swells the enthusiasm of the crowded marquee and, happy to be swept along, I press my outstretched hands into the air above me.

"I will praise you God! Yes I will praise you Lord."

I'm almost shouting the words now. Shouting down the doubts that revival is going to begin from anything I say. Shouting out the words as if every breath will somehow stockpile enough joy and love and lightness deep in my being to make an actual difference when I get back to school.

Because this time it needs to be different. The familiar post-camp blues encroach like the tide pulling with it the harsh, unchanging memories of previous September returns to school and my blatant failure to spark so much as one conversion to Christ, let alone a whole revival. In my mind it would have to be different this year. Now I was baptised in the Spirit. This September the return to school would be preceded by daily Spirit-filled prayer meetings with Julia, where we would sing and pray and claim our friends for Christ.

"Whenever two of you on earth agree about anything you pray for, it will be done for you by my Father in heaven."[1]

The words of Jesus popped into my mind and I stopped to search out the verse in Matthew's Gospel. Like a butterfly catcher with her net ready to snatch and pin down the gentle flicker of life, I pulled out the Bible highlighter crayon that Charlie had bought for me at the camp bookshop, and pressed down over the words with the seal of my pink crayon, clutching them as God's word to me.

"For where two or three come together in my Name, I am there with them."[2]

There. God would be with us, I planned, mentally working up my list of names of friends to convert. I pictured the kids spilling into the classroom that we would have to ask permission to use to house the lunchtime prayer meetings and Bible studies.

---

[1] Matthew 18.19.
[2] Matthew 18.20.

I knew too that there would be some potentially tricky politics, which Satan would no doubt use to thwart the move of God. I had been chucked out of the school Christian Union in my first year at Bournside, which was far more painful for my Dad than it was for me, given that it had been his stipulation that I should join in the first place. It turns out that a Monday lunchtime spent in Mrs Spenser's home economics classroom reading through the Book of Hebrews with three other kids and four teachers is indeed the kiss of death to an eleven-year-old, even a Bible-believing, Hell-avoiding one like me. Given that I was there under orders, my only escape seemed to be to make the best of the situation and at least see how far I had to go to provoke inappropriately timed explosions of laughter from Julia. The prayer time was usually the best moment, when everyone had their eyes closed.

"Dear God, we know that it says in the Book of Hebrews that you will judge your people and that it is a terrifying thing to fall into the hands of the living God. But I pray that you would let me fall into the hands of someone more handsome, less terrifying and with a better sense of humour."

But the only hands I fell into were those of Mr Deakes, the geography teacher, who, too nervous to enjoy a sense of humour, asked me to stop coming until I felt less destructive of other people's walk with the Lord.

Now the Lord was going to hear my prayers and answer with revival. I would put all gloating aside, as befits the leader of a campus of souls being awakened to the Good News of Jesus Christ. And I would invite Mrs Spenser and Mr Deakes and their Christian Union to join us in the music hall where we'd most likely have to move once the classroom became too crowded.

"Here in the grace of God I stand."

Kim's crooning repetition of the last line began her wrap-up, signalling to Peter Cabot and his ministry team that it was time to give space for the Holy Spirit to move upon us children. Instinctively we moved our bodies to tune in with this shift in tempo, lowering our raised hands down to the space in front of us, which may have looked as if we were all now holding the world's longest baguette, but was really showing God that we were ready to receive what He had for us.

And I wanted everything He'd got.

Prophecy.

Healing.

Visions.

Words of Knowledge.

Praying in tongues was just the start, the tangible evidence I needed to prove that I was chosen to do even greater things than Jesus.

But the uncomfortable corollary to all of my stretched-out, open-armed zeal was the calculation – the fear – that if God didn't show up and heal the sick, spark revival and meet my prayerful demands, then I wasn't in The Plan. It would signal some undiagnosed sin blocking the flow of the Holy Spirit through the vessel I was trying to be. It would show that I'd failed even to have faith the size of a mustard seed, which was all the faith Jesus said he needed to work with. And so I would come to heaven and discover that a mountain of unconfessed sin festering within me would consign me to the outer darkness where there is wailing and gnashing of teeth.

So, as the lightness of being in which camp had bathed us gave way to heavy dread about my absence from the Book of Life, I steeled myself for the return to school, where I prayed that the ridicule of teeth would be replaced by awe-struck acceptance of the Gospel I was about to proclaim.

8

Poisoned Pens

As it turned out, it wasn't from the darkness of school that the fresh onslaught of bullying came. It was the church youth group. Which is perhaps why, when an envelope addressed to me appeared in the Bible I'd left lying on the floor under a discarded pizza box, I sensed no danger.

Inside the envelope was a piece of paper torn out of a blue notebook with a scrawl of green felt-tip words across it, *"Can Opener! You are so ugly why don't you just kill yourself."* There wasn't a question mark because it wasn't a question, rather a conclusion calling time on any right I thought I had to partake in life's pleasures. I was not to belong in the same way as the others, even here in this church youth group where the author of the letter clearly existed. The pizzas, the midnight hikes through the Cotswolds, the camping trips and parties: these were not for me because these were about the space to blossom and reveal yourself and find as you did so that you could connect with other people and be discovered by them and, hopefully, eventually, be loved. But this person had written to tell me there was no point in me being involved in all that life and flourishing: it wasn't for me.

Later I stuffed the note into a box of letters and pushed it to the back of my wardrobe. Perhaps the letter might have been God's way of leading me out of temptation and delivering me from evil. So for a few brave days I tried to embrace this line of explanation. "Be thankful," I admonished myself in hollow moments on the way to school, in French lessons, and during cold cross-country runs, "surely this is God keeping you safe from sin. Just keep being thankful. You are set apart, Joanna, set apart for Him. You knew it would never feel comfortable."

Then the next letter arrived, blasphemously poked into the pages of my Bible again. I was too tired to convince myself it was the hand of God. And so when, a couple of weeks later, Debbie and Dave took us to a youth event in Birmingham, crammed with all the compelling ingredients you'd need for a high octane Christian youth rally, I finally combusted. All it took was the absence that evening of the boy who I knew must have written it, some loud music and the anonymity of slipping into the stream of other teenagers making their way to the front of the stage in response to an emotional altar call. The fact that the invitation was to unsaved teenagers to ask Jesus into their lives was neither here nor there. Now I was ready to initiate a conversation with God and issue Him a very specific invitation to intervene in my life.

It was a tear-soaked prayer in which I haemorrhaged three or four years' worth of gagged sadness. It must have been rather alarming, and potentially disappointing, for the woman on the team who'd taken me for a would-be convert and come to kneel beside me to prayerfully witness my conversion. I don't remember her saying a lot, but I do remember telling her and God that if God wanted to He could just come and make the braces fall off my teeth and put my teeth and jaws straight without all this hassle of head-braces and train-tracked teeth.

He could just do it.

Now. If You wanted to God, You could!

I really believed that He could.

But God was taking the long way round as God so often tends to do.

9

The First Leaf

Everyone needs to find their thing, especially in their teens. This is when you become able to have your thing that isn't your parent's thing or your teacher's, and possibly not even your friend's. It is yours, like your Unique Selling Point, with which you want to make your own mark on the world; the thing that will hoist you up on to the ladder of Becoming Someone. Which means, when you're a teenager, that it's almost instinctive to start building your brand with the way you look. Because when you're a young woman beauty is about the only thing you possess in bucketloads over everyone else. And it's the thing that most quickly and easily provokes a good reaction: replenishing one's emotional cache with affirmation.

At fourteen, perhaps even at 35, we don't necessarily make these calculations consciously. We somehow just know that we need to have our USP: that spark of something that sets us apart from the rest so that we are seen and loved. In a culture of consumerism and celebrity worship, the niche carved out for women to inhabit is physical perfection. And it's in the youthful bloom of teenage years that girls possess this power more than any others, at least commercially.

But of course commercial truth isn't the whole truth, because at fourteen it's a little early to expect you to embody the beauty that comes through loving or being loved, or through gathering up your creative instincts and shaping something prophetic and adding your voice to the world. Or by birthing your baby and incessantly pouring yourself out in love for this child, until your spirit is expanded more than you knew imaginable by the sacrifices you would make for this little person. At fourteen your beauty isn't dappled and worn by the failures you've overcome to make your contribution, and by the risks you've taken to try again. So at fourteen you do what you can to inhabit a worthy place in the world. You listen to the celebrity parroting "because you're worth it" and you buy the product that promises to deliver thick, glossy hair. Which is really problematic if your hair still feels like loft insulation, even after investing in that shampoo.

But even with the shampoo I was not going to be worth it … not in a commercial way. I tried to imagine that I had the face of a tanned, blue-eyed brunette from the Next catalogue, but still boys laughed in my face, my tormentors assailed me in the loos and two more poison-pen letters came my way. I needed to find a different USP, an alternative dressing-up box from which to manufacture some brand appeal. And so the exiled part of me began to calculate that as long as I had Some Thing, some useable currency, I wouldn't be left out and abandoned.

So, setting aside my longing for the armour of glossy hair and pretty make-up, I dutifully picked up my Bible and got on with trumping all that with the unfading beauty of eternal salvation. My USP was the Good News, the priceless possession that I would peddle to gain friends whilst assuaging the wrath of God and securing my place in heaven.

Naturally, I didn't know that this was the heavy mantle I was pulling onto myself. Perhaps we rarely know, until we learn one day to overhear ourselves. Until then we embrace the game of dressing up; we pick things out and, finding what is within our reach, we wrap them around ourselves, adjusting them until we have covered our vulnerable, embarrassing bits and feel sufficiently clothed. At fourteen years old you're beginning to try on roles and see if they fit; you're figuring out how believable you can be and how far your powers of influence actually go. But I had the voice of God on my side and surely that would boom louder than the lampooning of my persecutors. And so, with all the self-righteousness I could muster, I set out to fish souls for Jesus.

I began with Louise, one of the girls in my class with whom I'd been friends since we were six. At least our familiarity would mean I could skip any clumsy attempts to bring up out of the blue the subject of Jesus as my personal Lord and Saviour. Louise already knew, from first-hand experience at a Saturday night sleepover at my house, that church was the main feature of Sunday mornings in the Jepson household. She also knew that the most striking thing about our church was the worship leader: a man with cream sandals and a rainbow-coloured guitar strap who led the congregation in song whilst doing the holy hop, a dance move reminiscent of 1970s charismatic Christians. Which all basically meant, when I asked her if she fancied coming to church with me on Sunday, I knew the answer would probably be No.

It was No, but at least she cushioned it with a polite excuse. Under my breath I prayed for the right words to say something that would make church seem more attractive than spending the morning with her friends recovering from a late night at Smokey Joe's. But she anticipated my extension of the invitation to the evening church service instead.

"I'm going to St Mary's with Kitty on Sunday evening."

Darn. This was a sideways move. St Mary's was a traditional church.

"Oh OK, that's cool."

It wasn't cool. St Mary's was way too dull to spark a revival.

"So do you go with Kitty every week?"

"No, but the youth group are going to Cornwall on holiday this summer and I'm going too. We're all getting together after the service to do some planning."

"So … it's not that you've become a Christian then?"

"Well. I am … a Christian", Louise hesitated, wondering which criteria she should use to qualify her answer. "I've been baptised and we do go to church sometimes."

They had prepared us for this at camp, this way that people replace a personal relationship with God with a church attendance claim, and they had given me the words to say in response.

"But Lou, just because I go to McDonald's, it doesn't make me a hamburger."

"I don't get what you mean." Furrowing her eyebrows Louise screwed her mouth to one side and waited for my theological explanation.

This was it. At last. *Lord please help me to explain this right.*

"It's just that going to church doesn't make you a Christian. Following Jesus is about your whole life, not just Sundays. It's about knowing that Jesus loves you and has a good plan for your life, if you will only accept Him as Lord and be born again."

"I do believe in God though", she said slowly, with puzzled concern.

The words of Peter Cabot retorted in my mind, "The Devil believes in God too." But I softened the tone as I delivered his neat one-liner to Louise.

"So what are you saying? That I'm no better than the Devil?"

A fine mist of nausea was creeping across the depths of my stomach. In my trawl for Louise's soul the tangles of truth and doctrine began to twist, clenching me in their grip. The ungovernable waters of evangelism threatened to pull me overboard and drown me.

"It's just that God doesn't want you to end up on the side of the Devil. He loves you so much and wants to have a relationship with you … not just in this life but in heaven too." I hoped that the heaven bit might add some gravity to what was at stake here.

"So basically I'm going to go to hell if I don't become a born-again Christian?"

I looked down at the grass and the hefty tufts my fingers were tugging out of the ground between us.

Louise's face was down-turned too, which is why I didn't immediately look up and see her crying. It was as she reached for her bag and began rummaging around for some tissues that I saw her crumpled dismay breaking into tears.

St Paul warned us that the Gospel is foolishness to those who are perishing, but I just made my friend cry. There wasn't an immediately obvious passage of scripture to direct my response to this.

"Louise! Oh no … ! What is it?"

"What about Jess and Suzy? What if they don't want to be born again? Are you really saying God's going to send them to hell because … because … believing in God and going to church once a month isn't enough?"

If the free gift of eternal life was the bait then it was certainly beginning to take on the stomach-retching appeal of a tubful of crawling maggots.

"*Yes that's right*", Peter Cabot was whispering in my head. "*It doesn't matter if they believe in God – at the end of the day it's only Jesus who can save, only Jesus who took our sins to the cross, and only Jesus who rose from the dead, victorious.*"

"Lou, please don't cry … I'm sorry. I'm sorry."

Fisherman overboard.

"It doesn't matter that you're sorry ... it matters that what you said is true and my sisters might end up in hell."

"I know it sounds hard but ... but I know God doesn't want them to go to hell either. He wants to save them."

It didn't matter. We were both sinking and right now I didn't know how to save either of us.

"It's OK for you, your whole family are religious ... they're all going to heaven. You don't have to choose."

But I did have to choose. In my efforts to stop false doctrine bleeding into my carefully cradled judgements I was choosing all the time.

Right or wrong.

Friendship with God or friendship with the world.

Love of God or love of life.

So in that moment, with the nausea rising in my throat, I tried to cover my back and haul myself out of the deep.

"I suppose God may be calling you to be the one to share Jesus with your family. This might be His plan, Lou ... maybe you are the one to give them the choice."

It was a pitiful deflection and I was cringing with shame as the bell rang calling us to the safety of tutor group registration. I could, of course, have imagined that it was the Devil's fault and blamed him for skewering my evangelistic efforts. But not even the Devil deserved to be scapegoated for this.

10

Not God's: Mine

My USP had failed to sell Jesus and had failed to buy me friends, but most of all it troubled me that the Good News didn't really seem like good news at all. I tried to push aside this potentially blasphemous conclusion with more prayer and quell the fear that my bad PR was setting back the cause of Christ. So when, in those weeks of half-hearted prayer times and Bible studies with Jane, some actual good news landed on my radar, I was ready to be distracted.

I had had braces for the past three years and now my orthodontist, Mr Cooke, was trying a new tactic to train my lower jaw into a more normal position. This time two pieces of thick clear plastic were set onto wire which fixed around my teeth and dovetailed together like a jigsaw puzzle to hold my lower jaw forward. If evangelism had felt hard it was going to be nothing compared to the challenge of forming words with what was effectively two bricks of Duplo in the way. Under the glare of the examination light, I lay with my eyes closed, day-dreaming, while Mr Cooke wrestled my teeth into the wire frames. Finally he managed to snap the last awkward stretch of wire over my back tooth and sat back thumping his palms on his lap in satisfaction. I was busy running my tongue around the edges of this new oral furniture when Mum made her enquiry. "How long are we looking at this being in place then?"

"Well, if she's diligent and keeps it on every day then we could be looking at a year."

He brushed his hand through the sweep of hair that had fallen across the frame of his glasses, and peered at me.

"That's the thing though … You've got to do the work. You've *got* to wear it."

Mum eyed me, trying to work out if I'd taken the seriousness of this instruction on board or whether she was going to have to add her own encouragement.

"Guiii gouwm mmtttooo."

I tried to insist I would, but the neat arrangement of the jigsaw collapsed as I opened my mouth and I immediately leant forward to spit out the apparatus.

Mr Cooke had seen it all before. Reaching firmly for my chin and pulling me upright he brought the mirror down so that it was in front of my face.

"Now look in here." He deftly replaced the wayward lower brace.

"Take a look at that. Do you see what's going on? You've got to stay upright so that this upper brace can get purchase on the lower one."

I stared at my open mouth. The plastic might have been clear but there would be no hiding it from anyone. My lips framed a salivary jumble of teeth, wire and plastic and I began trying to reassemble it with my tongue.

"What happens after a year? Won't the bones begin to move back again?" Mum probed, her face still watching the orchestrations reflected in the mirror.

"It is going to be a temporary solution", Mr Cooke replied, his eyebrows raised in concession to Mum's thoughts.

"Ultimately we will be looking at a surgical reconstruction in her late teens, once the bones have fully stopped growing."

"Surgery?"

I spat the lower brace out again and swung round to face him.

He wasn't immediately sure whether I was about to dissolve into tears, the way I had when he told me at the age of eleven that I had to wear a head-brace.

But I didn't want to cry. I wanted to hug him.

All these braces were just salvaging the best from a bad situation. They were essentially rearranging the furniture inside a badly proportioned house. A house that I assumed I was stuck in. And here was Mr Cooke saying that one day they would be able to knock down that house and rebuild it properly. It didn't matter that I was going to have to wait two years for preparatory surgery and another two years after that for the main series of operations.

I stared at my face in the mirror, replaying Mr Cooke's words over and over; "*surgical reconstruction*". This was hope. It was a tangible alteration; a date in the diary. A goal which Mr Cooke and I would begin working towards. It wasn't like prayer, where I tried so hard to manufacture faith while all the time dreading the moment at which I would open my eyes and find that nothing had changed and God hadn't shown up. These operations I really could believe in.

When I got back to school later that morning, I sat at my desk daydreaming about the new squarer jaw Mr Cooke had promised. At lunchtime I wanted to tell Julia and Louise but found the task of eating sandwiches whilst holding onto the plastic blocks demanded all my concentration. My diligence lasted all of two mouthfuls before I grabbed a napkin and, leaning forward to click the wire out with my tongue, I abandoned my lunch.

"I've got something else to tell you ..."

Julia took a quick swig of juice and then set the bottle down on the desk in front of her expectantly.

"I'm going to have surgery! To put my teeth and jaw bones straight."

This might have been the kind of moment when adolescent girlfriends disingenuously pretend that there's nothing wrong with you, that you're fine, that you don't need surgery. But neither of them did.

"Seriously?" Louise said in quiet astonishment.

Before I could answer, Julia burst in, "What do you mean? What are they going to do?"

"Well, I have to wait a few years ... but basically they're going to cut a strip of bone out of my top jaw and then break all the way along my lower jaw and slide half of it forward, pin it together ... and then build me a chin."

It was the end of this sentence that caught nearby Victoria and Lizzie's attention and produced a half-smiling incredulity from them both. "Build you a chin?" Victoria swung herself around from the chair she'd been sitting in and leant over the desk to await full details.

"I've just been to the orthodontist ... it looks like they can sort out my jaw problem with surgery. When I've stopped growing."

"So how long do you have to wait for that then?" Lizzie asked.

"I think it's going to be when I'm nineteen or maybe even twenty."

"Oh my god, Joanna, that's years!"

"Won't it be very painful? It sounds horrendous."

"Are you going to have braces until then?"

The questions were raining down now.

"What about your religion?" Louise's question caught me. "Are you allowed to do that sort of thing?"

It was funny how she had thought of it before me. Following God's no-show at the National Exhibition Centre youth rally last year I had taken the matter out of God's inbox and no longer saw it as His jurisdiction. Now that Mr Cooke had taken charge and was making some tangible progress, it hadn't occurred to me that I might have to resubmit it for a divine veto.

Over supper that evening Mum and I relayed Mr Cooke's prognosis to Dad, Ali and Rosalind.

"Goodness me, darling," Dad exclaimed, turning from Mum to me, "we're talking about major surgery here."

I sat waiting, trying to second guess what my parents' response was actually going to be.

"It is major, John. It's going to mean a spell in intensive care, at least two weeks in hospital and several weeks with her jaws wired together."

"Oh darling." Dad winced and rubbed his hand across his jaw.

"Do you really want to go through all that?" Rosalind questioned matter-of-factly. "Why don't you just stick with braces?"

"The braces aren't going to straighten everything out really … not my bones anyway."

She put down her knife as the potential implications of my situation began to dawn on her. "Am I going to have to have surgery too, Mum?"

"No, I think you're going to be OK with just a brace for a little while."

"I don't want brace!" said Alastair, taking his place in the family discussion.

"I thought you wanted braces like me, Ali?" I protested, nudging him.

"No! I'm not. I don't want it! Urgh!" He shuddered to underline his reluctance.

Rosalind looked across the table to me: "Why do you have to have an operation then?"

"Because I can't close my mouth properly without it …"

"Have you really thought about whether it's worth all that pain just to be able to close your mouth?" Dad was almost pleading with me now.

"Urgh! Urgh! I don't want it! Urghhhhh!" Ali was now working his dislike of braces into a full drama of hammed-up distress. His outstretched hands, shaking in mock disgust, knocked my knife onto the floor, splattering food as it fell.

This kind of dinnertime fracas was typical, but that evening I was on edge; all the tabletop antics were encumbered with the weight of the bigger matter of surgery. The subject was allowed to drift for the remainder of the meal until Rosalind and Ali had left the table and there was peace enough to talk.

"Have you thought it through, sweetheart?"

"John, she only found out about it this morning … she's got years to go before anything happens."

"Well I think I should come to your next appointment and hear what Mr Cooke has to say."

"But what about what I have to say?"

"Well, tell me … what do you think about it?"

"I want to have the operation. I definitely do."

"You've got time to think about it", Mum interjected, trying to pace me.

"Why? Don't you think I should go through with it?" I hadn't altogether managed to work out what Mum thought.

"I do. But it's OK for you to change your mind."

"Didi! Do you really want her to go through that? With all your nursing, you know better than anyone what it will entail …" Dad was dismayed.

"But Dad, why don't you want me to do it?"

"Because I don't want to see you suffer."

There was a pause. I wasn't thinking of what to say, I was just trying to hold the words back as long as I could.

Then I said it, very quietly. "But I'm suffering now."

It was the closest I had come to letting them know what things were like for me because of my face, and I didn't want to let them get any closer, so I got up and walked towards the hallway.

"Joey," Mum called after me, "why don't you spend some time praying about it?"

Afterwards, I didn't pray about it.

I lived in a home where everything we owned was considered a blessing from the Lord; where God was brought into every decision and everything we did was submitted to the Lordship of Christ. When it came to choosing subjects at school things like sociology and psychology were off-limits, considered too liberal for a girl raised to know that Jesus was the Way, the Truth and the Life. When I asked to do something, like having my ears pierced, Mum and Dad would tell me to ask the Lord whether I should, which was really just them giving me a chance to hear God's No, before theirs; because generally God seemed to be against stuff.

Top of the Pops, swearing, fornication, make-up, wizards, shopping on Sundays and taking too much interest in material things: they were all frowned upon if not entirely ruled out. Which meant Rosalind and I didn't really need to pray about things because we got a sixth sense about the things God was going to be OK with. Things like tithing, spending time at church or youth group or any other Christian gathering, and television programmes like *Highway to Heaven* and *Songs of Praise*. And pierced ears; in the end God didn't mind too much about that either.

Now here was an epic, life-changing, life-giving possibility on which there was no clear biblical guidance. And it was mine. It wasn't a parental edict that I had to obey; it wasn't money that could be tithed; it wasn't virginity that I was compelled to pledge to some far-off ideal of a husband. Mr Cooke had given me a choice and it was my decision to make. I couldn't now risk offering this up in prayer only for God to come and lash through my hope with His No. It didn't belong to Him.

Perhaps it wasn't strange that this promise of cutting and splicing, of breaking and remoulding, felt so whole. Its presence way ahead in the unlived days of 1995 became a shelter from the assaults as I journeyed through the rest of 1991 ... 92 ... 93 ... 94 ... What I couldn't yet acknowledge were the splits and denials that my half-beliefs in God were causing. The thought of my attempts to convert people, the image of Louise's tears and my inability to make the Good News good, curdled in my memory. The fear of God and what His wrath would do to me if I failed to live up to this good Christian life: these were the distorted untruths that fractured me. To give them voice would be like knowing the answer is 7 but admitting to the teacher that somehow you keep calculating 3.9. All I'd ever been told was that God is love and God is good, but all I now heard and absorbed were threats of where we'd end up if we didn't mirror that goodness in our lives. So I lingered, silently, with the wounds of fear and confusion that these jagged edges of half-truth and twisted dogma had left, not realizing that, unacknowledged, they would soon become infected.

Out of all the games of "Hot or Not" going on in my world, Christianity operated the least attractive one. Who thought that threats of eternity spent in outer darkness would be the message of love to compel unbelievers to believe? How did our Christian leaders not see that it would simply plant the seeds of cynicism and unbelief in our own young minds? We were burdened with The Truth and told to take it to the nations in the Name of Jesus, but nobody stopped to tell us that judgement of mortal souls was never ours to make. And so we carried on doing our best to slap the sticking-plasters of truth onto the cuts our words of proclamation had inflicted. "So it says in the Bible that I'm going to go to hell unless I believe that Jesus is the Way, the Truth and the Life?" my prey would ask. "Yes, but Jesus has died and risen to save you from that destiny ... as long as you accept him."

I wonder if Eve, having taken and eaten the forbidden fruit, suddenly found herself trying to appropriate the complexities of all her newly acquired knowledge. Did she struggle to handle these frightening new layers of good and evil, which could only ever be held by the wise omnipotent God? Standing on the sidelines of the Genesis story I hear myself shouting at her, "Turn around! Turn around! Stop hiding; stop trying to manage it all by yourself ... You can tell God ... Don't be afraid ... Remember the love and just tell Him!"

Love is, after all, what we want.

But she didn't return to that love because, overtaken by confusion, she tried to find her salvation in knowledge, instead of letting love hold and remind her.

Such fear and confusion had also overtaken me. Fear that I wasn't really saved, and that I had irrevocably flouted God's love by not demonstrating enough faith for Him to minister through me. But, if someone was shouting from the sidelines at me, "Turn around! You don't have to hold all this together ... Just tell God ... He understands ... He loves you! Don't be afraid!", I didn't hear them and battled on trying to prove to God that I could handle what I mistakenly thought He required of me.

Like Adam and Eve, trying to digest the kind of knowledge that was only truly safe in God's hands, I messily regurgitated the dogmatic truths that I wasn't big enough to contain.

11

Kafir and Caliphates

It might have been a much cleaner process if I'd just tried to understand St Paul's theology, given that most New Testament threats seemed to emanate from him. But I decided I would find little sympathy for any question or challenge of the man whom preacher-men seemed – unaccountably – to rave about. I didn't want to get into trouble for being disruptive at Sunday school, so I tried to muster enthusiasm for the positive bits where he didn't appear too ranty. And I tried to ignore just how conflicted I felt about my need to make it into his heavenly gang. Because we all need a gang, right? And when you're desperate to get into a gang, there's nothing quite as reassuring as someone pointing out those who aren't in it.

I was used to people pointing out that I wasn't in the popular gang, and I was used to preacher-men pointing out who wasn't in God's gang: people who campaign for shopping on Sundays; people who have sex before marriage; people who think they're a good person and don't need to invite Jesus into their hearts; homosexuals and Muslims.

The memory of a preacher-man at camp years before, standing on the main stage loudly declaring that the Muslims were waiting to rise up and take over the UK and establish their Islamic

Caliphate, had carved its way into my worldview. It was another one of those adult meetings that I probably shouldn't have gatecrashed. Living in Cheltenham, where there weren't many Muslims, made the prospect even more sinister because it seemed they must all be hiding somewhere out of sight, watching us, just waiting for their moment to take over the nation. So it was a shock when, that summer, we arrived at Good News Crusade to find we were sharing the showground with an Islamic youth camp.

As we drove through the main gate entrance, all hot and dishevelled in our non-air-conditioned car, we immediately noticed the long, high fence that had been erected to the side of the main track. Where we expected to see the familiar arrangement of Big Top, Power Pack, Salt Pot and bookshop tents, there was a large square marquee and behind it two smaller rectangular tents. The field, where we spent our evenings lolling around with chips and a ghetto-blaster, was now unfamiliar with the sight of dark skinned, kufi-capped boys and further away, behind another fence, a large crowd of robed girls, the edges of their veils lifting in the breeze.

"Hello! What's all this?" Mum wound down her window as Dad slowed the car and leaned across her to get a better view.

"What have they done with our camp?" Rosalind piped up, clutching the top of the open window with both hands.

Dad slowed the pace to 5mph while he surveyed their camp.

"I don't believe it. They're on our field", I cried.

"Who are they? They're not part of GNC!"

"They've gone and rented out half the camp to Muslims by the looks of things", he said, gently accelerating.

"Didi, we're going to have to watch Alastair closely. As far as he's concerned that's where his youth meetings take place."

"Girls, do you hear me? You need to make sure that you stick with AJ to and from meetings until he's got the hang of the new layout."

"Oh goodness", Mum murmured. "I hope we don't lose him in there."

For Alastair the religious divisions, demarcated by fence and doctrine, would find little purchase in his mind. It was the rest of us in whom the defences of suspicion and prejudice and exclusion took root. Now we had something besides demons to intrigue us. Each day Charlie, his friend Russell, Katie, Julia, Hannah and I would gather by the fence to watch the goings on beyond the wire. "Do you remember John Barton saying that the Muslims were going to rise up and take over Britain?" I asked Charlie.

"No. John Barton hasn't been at camp for years. When did he say that?"

"It was years ago, in one of the Big Top meetings."

"What do you think they do over there?" Katie was sitting cross-legged in front of the fence, chewing a piece of grass, her fingers absent-mindedly twiddling round the wire.

"They don't sing, they don't play games: what's their camp for?"

"To prepare them to rise up and take over the UK when they grow up ...", Charlie smirked.

"It might be. They don't seem to be having any other fun."

"Yeah, they're separated from the girls for a start", Russell murmured out of the corner of his mouth.

"I wish we could talk to them and find out what they're doing." Katie looked over her shoulder at me, hoping to find a partner in crime. Charlie was having none of it.

"How do you think that would go, Kate? For a start you're a girl. They're not going to go anywhere near you."

But they did come near us, or at least two of them did, because it turned out that they were just as intrigued about the noise that came from our camp as we were about the lack of noise from theirs. As we stood pressed up against the fence trying to coax the two lads to come closer and talk to us, they stayed a little way off, nervously looking over their shoulders and talking in low voices between themselves.

I leaned over to Charlie. "They're not going to take over anything with that kind of attitude."

Charlie called out to them gently, "Hey, hey, can you come and talk to us? Go on … we just want to say hello and have a chat …"

They took a few paces towards us, and one of them called back, "What are you lot doing?"

"Trying to talk to you."

"But what are you doing at your camp?"

"Is it true that you're religious?" the other one cut in.

"We're at Good News Crusade, it's a Bible camp."

"So you're Christians?"

"Yes!" We all chipped in, nodding.

"What are you doing?" I couldn't wait any longer to find out.

"Muslim youth camp."

"Yeah but what do you do all day?"

"We learn the Koran … pray … learn the teachings of the Prophet, peace be upon him."

"So … er … are you having a good time?" I asked, unable to tell whether this translated into the kind of socializing that our own week of religious teaching and worship allowed.

"Joey!" Charlie jabbed his elbow in my ribs. But the boys didn't answer, they just nervously checked over their shoulders to see if anyone had noticed them.

"Why aren't you allowed to talk to us?"

"You're kafir."

"What's that?" I retorted, pretty sure that I was nothing of the sort.

"You're unbelievers ..."

"We're not ... we definitely believe."

"We're Christians."

"We shouldn't be talking to you", the other one said, more for the benefit of his friend.

"Because we're Christians?"

"You're not going to convert anyone if you don't talk to us." The flippancy of his words told me that Charlie was now warming up for some fun.

"Are you worried that we might try and convert you?" I asked them, trying to wrestle the conversation from his mischief.

"You can't convert us." He spoke defiantly, thrusting his chin up as he did so; then he turned to his friend and they spoke in low voices again.

"Well, you can't convert us either ... But we still want to talk to you." I added that so as not to appear unfriendly.

But he ignored me and looked at Charlie and Russell, "Yeah, so ... what do you do at your camp then?"

I felt perfectly able to answer and there was no need for the boys to do all the talking, but from across their field came a distant shout. A voice raised, calling out in our direction. The boys turned and hurried away towards the voice, and we stood there for a few moments before realizing that the sight of us all pressed up against the fence watching was probably going to give them away.

"Let's come back later and see if they're here again", Katie persisted, feeling she'd not got a full enough picture of what a week at Islam Camp had to offer.

During the afternoon I thought about our certainties, about each of our claims to be Believers and how confidently all of us would deny that each other was a Believer also. I thought about how easily we thought we knew better than them: that they weren't believers but sadly deceived teenagers who didn't have the hope of salvation like we did. Which meant that I didn't feel so entitled to be angered by their dismissal of us as kafir, but nevertheless I was. What did they know? How dare they? They were so blinded by the half-truths of Islam! Goodness, it would be more or less impossible to convert them. And I began to think about which verses of scripture I would start with if I were going to try.

Through the afternoon's praise and worship I sat thinking of scriptures about Jesus dying and rising to new life and how I would use them to win this brewing faith-off. But if it were that straight-forward to tell them our Jesus story then evangelism would be easy and I would always be on the winning side.

What I couldn't see that afternoon was that this was no faith-off, because it wasn't about faith. Not on their side of the fence, nor on ours. The twisted metal confining each of us within the limits of religious truth was hammered and held in place by pillars of other people's fears and hopes. These leaders, parents, preachers, imams who had brought us to our various sides of the fence had done so because they wanted us to take on their beliefs. They wanted to shape our souls and minds along the angles of their belief, and deepen the roots of our character in the ground of their doctrines. They wanted us to shoulder their religion so that we, too, would help them remake the world around us in the same mould. It was an evolutionary instinct shored up by a muddle of love and cultural politics.

You want to protect your children and keep them safe from moral corruption or eternal suffering, you want to give them knowledge of a love that goes beyond the reach of any protection you could ever provide for them. This is the faith you want to give them. But children can never be repositories of their parents' faith – for faith cannot be imposed. Its exhilaration can only be experienced at the point of heart-leaping, mouth-gulping risk. Instead we were being removed from the possibility of faith, removed from risk to the safety of a place where questions would be met with firm answers and desires bridled by strict moral codes. But they didn't yet see that they were setting us up to come to the riskiest place of all, where we might have to break through all the architecture of their anxiety and indoctrination and, beyond the splintered mess, find faith for the first time.

When we returned to our grassy spot later that evening we were disappointed at first to find that all was quiet on the other side of the wire. It was only after a little while that I noticed the white of their clothing standing out against the dark trees, moving slowly near the far fence. "What are they doing?"

The others all swivelled to follow my pointing finger. We each began to move back to the fence again to see properly. Slowly, the two figures moved closer along the far perimeter so that we could see them.

"What are they doing?" Katie echoed my words as the rest of us stood silently trying to compute what we were seeing.

It was them: the boys we'd been talking to. Hands behind their heads, crawling on their knees like unwilling pilgrims around the half-mile circumference of the fence.

"Is that because of us?"

No one spoke.

"Probably", Charlie finally replied, sombrely. "Their leaders are probably trying to send us a message."

"Is that even allowed?"

"I feel sick."

"Let's call Childline."

"We can't, no one's going to come and get them out of there. And even if they did, then what? That's their religion."

"But it's awful."

It took a long time for them to crawl their way past our small section of wire but even in the darkening twilight we didn't want to risk their imams seeing them, so we lay down like soldiers lying in wait. Eventually the boys inched their way past, leaving several feet of space between themselves and us. We hissed loudly to them. "Are you OK?"

"Is there anything we can do?"

But their faces, contorted in discomfort and shame, were focused on each new patch of lumpy grass beneath their knees.

"We're so sorry", I whispered.

Suddenly our God didn't seem so wrathful, or so insecure, needing to crash down upon our attempts to reach out with cruel punishment. What was it that their imams were so afraid would happen? Could their idle chatter with kafir really wrest away their hearts and minds from Allah? It seemed that their leaders had more faith in our faith than I did.

12

Laying Out the Bodies

Perhaps it is strange that Islam's covering of female faces and bodies didn't appeal to me; that I didn't look across that field at the girls behind fences and veils and wish that I had that kind of relief or protection from unwanted stares. But it didn't strike me as liberating, because it wasn't the kind of freedom I wanted. My heart and mind closed down towards these Muslim neighbours and I came away from the fence frustrated and angered by the harshness we'd seen. If Muslims were going to take over Britain then I should probably start taking world evangelism a bit more seriously again. Maybe I would be more successful as a novelty foreign missionary instead of just the weird class Bible-basher.

The problem was that old-school missionaries no longer existed; now you had to go to another country with a basic skill – something you could usefully do whilst waiting to meet people to share the Good News with. It wasn't at all clear what my skill might be. Dad certainly worried about it. Perhaps it was because of my school record, so blighted by bad-scoring maths and science results, that he hoped I would be good. If career options weren't going to be in plentitude then all the more reason to keep me on the straight and narrow and avoid any moral lapse to boot.

So a cursory glance at my school record didn't offer any promising options for a would-be missionary. Leaders at camp talked about their ministry travelling the world, seeing people become Christians and the sick healed and the possessed delivered. That was the kind of career I wanted to have. Except, as a girl, I wouldn't be able to be a preacher, unless I married a preacher man and then got invited to speak to women's groups. It didn't altogether matter that the Church of England had voted to ordain women and soon now Emmanuel Church would have a female priest; my parents were against it and so it wasn't floated as a suitable career path for me.

When the vote for the ordination of women had passed through General Synod, Julia, Vicky, Rachel, Liz and I had been sitting in the common room vaguely listening to the radio. As the Yes vote was relayed, Vicky commented that she might like to be a lady vicar. I was appalled. All I could think of was Vicky trussed up in a man's oversized, grey, clerical shirt and ugly shoes, having to engage in constant facial depilation to erase any signs of a beard. What an awful job for a woman. Being a missionary was far more adventurous and I could still wear women's clothes.

But, deep down, it wasn't really the call of the mission field that was burning within me; it was the escape that that would provide. I needed a future that would combine a worthy use of time with an exit from a life etched by poisoned pens and ferocious slanging about my face. Being a missionary or a Red Cross aid worker was the perfect option. It would take me to places in the world where it wouldn't matter what I looked like: orphans and war criminals wouldn't have the emotional energy to taunt me.

The question was: what was my basic skill going to be? Since it had taken three attempts to pass my maths GCSE, it was fair to strike engineering and medicine off the list immediately. That left teaching and nursing, but teaching would expose me to classrooms full of children and I'd had my fill of that already. Sick patients would be far more grateful. So nursing it was. I didn't pray about it. As far as I could see I didn't have the luxury of other options. God would have to take me or leave me. I applied to nursing colleges and finally persuaded one that I had what it took. My parents knew it was going to be a disaster, but they didn't tell me that.

I wonder exactly what kind of disaster they foresaw. Would it be my incomprehension of the fine-tuning of sugar intake necessitated by a diabetic patient, and my innocent offer of jam with their breakfast? Would it be my impatience that would see me launch in to deal with a haemorrhaging patient without pausing to grab surgical gloves? Or my absent-minded abandon of the drugs trolley in the corridor complete with used needles balanced on top … "until I could find the right bin, Matron".

I was indeed a disaster. In the lecture hall one afternoon I looked around at the other 104 students in my year and felt the discord of being the only person there who didn't really want to be a nurse. I needed to keep focus on the end goal and so I taped a picture of a poverty-stricken child from an Oxfam advertisement to the inside of my nursing file to remind me.

In the meantime, I tried to settle down with the other 22 girls with whom I was housed, in a long, wooden hut on stilts. Left over from some hurried post-war erection, its partition walls were thin plasterboard, too fragile, it seemed, to hold the weight of the heavy fire-doors; the whole corridor would shake when a group of us walked down the hallway together. If it looked dark and inhospitable from the outside the atmosphere within did not dispel that impression. Mainly because the glowering, sophisticated 21-year-old business studies student in the room next to me intimidated all of us meek 18-year-olds with her car, boyfriends and imperviousness to the need for friends.

While we were revelling in the excitement of daily visits to the student bar, Mara held cocaine-fuelled court in her room until 5 a.m. for doped-up third years and, clearly, utterly loathed being housed in the hut with naive school leavers like us. So it is difficult to know whether she made me the target of her disgruntlement because I was nearby or because I was the epitome of everything she resented.

But it got undeniably personal when at 4 a.m. one morning I heard the chatter coming from her room swerve in my direction.

"Don't worry about it," came her dismissive voice, "she's not doing shifts."

Then, after a moment of indiscriminate chatter, she continued,

"It's like living with fucking mice around here."

"You said she was a chipmunk."

"Oh my God. You've seen her right?"

"She looks like a fucking bent snow-plough."

Thwack, thwack, hammer.

She was bringing it to me. She wanted me to hear and to know.

The pictures on my wall rattled as her fist hammered against it.

"Get your fucking ear off my wall, bitch."

After half an hour I took my duvet and went to curl up on the floor in the bathroom until it was over.

The nightly pantomime involving pointed impersonations continued for a further few nights, disturbing other girls who asked with concern what was going on as we walked to the refectory for breakfast in the mornings. Alison offered to leave her door unlocked so I could let myself in and sleep on her floor when I needed, and the others wondered what Mara's problem was. I assumed that the drugs were doing the talking, which felt like a generous response but was just less frightening than acknowledging I was living next to a sociopath who enjoyed heaping misery on those around her. It was only the following weekend that it became clear that we were actually living with the deliberate ragings of a disturbed woman.

Mara sped off to the country that Friday afternoon and the whole block breathed sighs of relief, beginning to talk a bit more freely in the kitchen and discussing what kind of penalty could be slapped on her. We talked about getting a student liaison officer to come over and hear our complaints the following week. We sat up drinking cocoa, talking about boys and nursing, and planned a Saturday walk and pub lunch. We all went to bed reassured that nothing would wake us that night.

And nothing did, until 4 a.m. when my dream was slowly invaded by strange sounds. It continued working its way into the narrative of my unconsciousness, and then persisted until it took over, pulling me out of my dream with a vibration that sounded like expanding and contracting machinery. The radiator next to my bed was shaking, the fragile window, running wall to wall across the width of my room, was rattling, and so were the pictures on one wall – the wall I shared with Mara. From the other side of the plaster partition came the audible assault of discordant moans and sounds, too bizarre to be recognized as music. It died away and then started again. Over. And over. Its loudness concussed my attempts to decipher what I was hearing.

It went on for an hour, exactly. With the volume set to max, her alarm clock stereo had been timed to play '666' from *The Omen*. Set to repeat, its drone rose and died again and again, dragging us from our sleep. After several repeats I staggered out of my dark room and knocked on Alison's door. Other doors were beginning to open and weary faces appeared in hope of answers. Only Adele, from further along the corridor, recognized the sound from the horror film. We were suitably horrified. I tried Mara's door but it was locked. Alison stepped out of her doorway and around me to try and peer through the keyhole. Although it was dark she could see the pale lights of the stereo sat on the floor pressed up against the wall adjoining my room.

"What a bitch", her Lancashire accent softened the bluntness of her exclamation.

"She's turned her stereo towards Joanna's room."

"What?! Let me see." Judith pulled Alison back to get a look.

"I can't believe her. Why would she want to do something like that?"

"Oh God, can't we break her door down to make it stop?"

"I'm going to set the fire alarm off."

"No! Don't do that, JJ, you'll get kicked out if you set off a false alarm."

That struck me as a fitting way to bring the misery of my university existence to an end. But Adele took charge and, pulling a hoodie over her pyjamas, she slipped out to go and find the student accommodation liaison officer. The rest of us decided to retreat to the kitchen at the other end of the corridor and make tea with the placebic conviction that it would make everything feel much better. When, at 5 a.m., the noise suddenly stopped we sat silently looking at one another with relief.

Within a couple of weeks three girls had packed up their suitcases and moved to alternative accommodation, but the student nurses had to stay. Our placements were to begin a couple of months later and the college authorities wouldn't countenance our petition to move. Mara's presence seethed over our weekdays and for the next six Saturday mornings she continued to leave Satan's own soundtrack to shudder through our creaking rooms at 4 a.m. Out in our far corner of campus property, away from pay phones and liaison officers, nothing could stop the number of The Beast groaning and whining its eerie doom into our weekend slumbers.

It no longer mattered that we knew the music so well that the horror of surprise had now given way to sheer irritation that we were being regularly woken so early. I began to wake early anyway, my body anxiously jolting me in preparation to withstand a new round of assault. Even when sounds didn't come, because it was 3.15 a.m. on Tuesday morning, the contrails of dread wound slowly through my body. I lay there, aware that the alarm in my body would not switch off within an hour. The wretchedness heaved through my senses, ripping away the remaining threads of confidence and hope I had spent years trying to hold together.

Without the safety of a home to retreat to at the end of each day I withered fast. Making my way after supper each evening to the pay phone booth, I dialled my home number and let the voice of Mum or Dad catch the torrent of sobs erupting from deep within me. If it hadn't been for the nearby church with its lively group of young adults I would have sunk by Christmas. But in time this crowd gathered me up in their welcome and spontaneous adventures to climb Snowdon or camp on freezing Dorset beaches, or to hand out sandwiches to the homeless in London. Here I was welcomed and there was no viciousness to bar me.

Except on Monday morning the peace was gone. And so was my enthusiasm for nursing. My friends from church returned to their careers, while I limped through lectures on biology and first aid and diabetes and stared at the Oxfam child on the inside cover of my notes. Her little face was the only thing connecting me to the picture of my future that I had built up, and that was waiting for me in a far-off mission field. Every essay on the physiological process involved in vomiting or the treatment of bedsores reduced the dream to a drag of grinding irrelevancies, which I had little energy to learn. It was now eight months until the first major operation and it rose up before me on the horizon, the Alpha and Omega of my life's vision.

And this is a problem when you find yourself in church on a Sunday singing songs about Jesus being the centre of our life and the one for whom we lived.

It was blatantly disingenuous and Jesus knew, even if nobody else did, that Mr Harrison, my surgeon, was the first man on my mind, not just during church, but most of the time. He was the miracle-working genius to whom I was going to submit my face and my future. Not Jesus.

My utter focus on surgical renewal would have been understandable to most people, and even to God. But God doesn't settle for being merely understanding of our idols and addictions. And in the early weeks of 1995, as my church pastor talked about the story of Abraham and how God asked him to give up everything that mattered most to him and sacrifice even his son, I weighed heavily with the conviction that I must do the same.

At my next appointment in Cheltenham I dreaded telling Mr Harrison that I had changed my mind. A group of medical students were following me through this journey of orthodontic transformation and there was no easy moment to manhandle things from fifth gear into reverse. Which might be why I chose the most impossible moment to get Mr Harrison's attention: when his hand had clamped my teeth together and the metal ruler was being slid down the side of my jaw to get a precise reading of my overbite. I pushed the words out from inside my shut mouth. "I'm having second thoughts."

Out came the ruler and Mr Harrison looked down at me as if I'd reached an inevitable halt in this journey. Clipboards were lowered and everyone was sent out of the room. The nurse set her notes down and left too, while Mr Harrison flicked the switch to raise the chair so that I could look at him upright, face to face.

"Is it the risks involved?" he asked.

He seemed glad that I was taking the possibility of a severed facial nerve seriously. But it wasn't the idea of having a palsy; the possibility that the left side of my face might droop and my mouth drool forever. I squirmed slightly in the chair wondering how to bring the messiness of my theological angst into the sanitized order of his NHS clinic. How do you tell your doctor that you are conflicted by the fact that his handiwork has become your means of salvation and that it has become an idol that you have to let go of and relinquish? Silently I comforted myself with the devotion of my Abrahamic obedience and I insisted that the operations were off, hoping God was sufficiently appeased.

Mr Harrison assured me that I would remain in his diary of clinic appointments just in case this was a temporary falter of nerves. I agreed, knowing that there was no point because I'd truly let it go. As I walked through the car park to find Mum, my heart slumped with inertia at the now empty horizon ahead.

That afternoon, as Mum waved me off on the bus back to college, there were tears in her eyes as she thought about what I was returning to. My hospital placement had begun three days previously and I hated it. It only took three more weeks of my escalating liabilities on the ward for my nurse mentor to quietly begin giving me the dead bodies to lay out. It seemed safer for everyone. I was about to turn nineteen, and I wished I was one of those dead bodies.

In the evenings I walked around the ward sitting on the end of patients' beds for a chat, but the gentleness of those encounters, in which I brushed against their loneliness and fears, only made me feel my own more intensely and I couldn't stop my tears falling. The pummelling daily anxieties, whether on- or off-shift, twisted my stomach into knots and gnawed away at my resolve. Daydreams of Red Cross field hospitals became an end that the means rendered improbable. I didn't have what it takes to become a nurse, and was rapidly heading towards the status of patient. My throat began to constrict, tightening until I could no longer swallow food. One of the nurses started giving me build-up drinks from the patient's supplies but it was going to take more than calorific milkshakes to ward off the impending avalanche of unmitigated strain.

A week after my nineteenth birthday I collapsed. My parents jumped in the car and drove over to pack my bags and take me home.

13

Alastair

There was a mirror leaning up against the wall next to the window in my bedroom when I got home. The kind of unremarkable rearrangement that happens as parents' belongings begin to spill into the no-man's-land of a grown child's old bedroom. Alastair found me sitting cross-legged in front of it one evening and squeezed himself down into a crouch next to me while I studied this now gaunt face that, I'd overheard Grandma remark, "the light had gone out of." Nestling his face next to mine, Ali's eyes were alight with enthusiasm. He had his big sister home and all labels of *depression* and *nervous exhaustion* plastered upon me were meaningless to his mind. There was no worry for my health and future, only excitement and happiness that I was back where I ought to be, in the bedroom across the hall from his, to be reassuringly found each morning once he woke up and shuffled sleepily across the landing to climb onto the end of my bed while I drank my tea.

Now we looked into the mirror together, Alastair's hand cradling my head up against his face.

"Hey! Hey! Come and see … do we look like twins? You and me?"

I watched us in the mirror. "Do we look like twins?" I repeated, smiling.

"Yeah, go on! Are we twins?"

"We're not twins, Ali … I'm nineteen and you're seventeen!"

"But look. Go on!"

I looked. His eyes were alive with gleeful expectation. My eyes that had been almost permanently swollen from the daily outpouring of tears were now empty and pale, framed by dark shadows.

"Tell me I look like you."

"Do you want us to look like twins, Ali?"

"Yeah! You and me."

"But why, Ali? You're my brother we already do look like each other."

"Noooo." He frowned with frustration. Then he moved and kneeled up behind me in the mirror and looked at himself. Putting his dry, creased hands up to his ruddy cheeks, he pleaded with his reflection for a moment.

"I don't have Down syndrome face. I look like you."

In that late May evening sunlight Alastair's words suddenly toppled the weight of intrusive ugly labels under which I was now collapsed, depressed and crushed. Right now I was the picture of normality that my brother wanted to reflect. Resembling me was his validation. As we knelt there by the window, squeezed between a chair and the airing-cupboard door, the world outside was all at once forgotten in that image of brother and sister before us in the mirror. There we were, for a moment, unassailable by the shallow judgements of teens who'd fed for too long on a diet of celebrities and supermodels. Whole and complete, simply occupying the features that were ours: features that contained our storylines and bore the harmonies of belonging with each other. There was nothing else in that moment with which we could have been compared and pronounced defective.

I smiled at Alastair, yet I knew that it was the jibes and taunts of his own foes that made him insist that we could be as indistinguishable as twins. I leaned forward, looking at the architecture of my bones and teeth reflected before me. What would it be like to simply inhabit this face without letting the commentary of strangers reach beneath the layers of appearance and wring the life out of me? I looked at Alastair, noticing the facial creases and slants that were supposedly symptoms of his disability, but seemed only to form irrepressible expressions of mischief and frustration, joy and love.

I wanted to stand between him and the world, barring access to anyone who might bring their inadequacies and, even inadvertently, dump them on him. But that would deny the world Alastair.

Mum had said that he would make some people feel afraid. And in a strange way that was part of his gift, being able to lift the veil on people's pomp and pretence. Because when people were busy keeping up appearances Ali wouldn't fall for their good impressions. The workmen digging up the road in their high-vis jackets were no less exciting to talk to than the Bishop in all his robes. I guessed that Mum had been right when she told me about people's fears, because if people were trying to hide behind their cool exterior then Alastair could be a very risky person to know.

While the rest of us were chomping on that morsel of forbidden fruit hoping for a bellyful of satisfaction from playing God over everyone else, that bite of fruit was never properly digested by Ali. Where we might fall over ourselves trying to suck up to the eminent and successful, Alastair remained somehow blind.

Disabled? You betcha! He was out there living his life without the same armour the rest of us fashion for ourselves. It left him naked and an easy target for those who might be shown up by his lack of pretence. It wasn't that he denounced or mocked people's power plays, it's just that that wasn't what he responded to in people. When we might notice someone else's brilliance and translate that into a judgement about our own inadequacy, or when someone else's badness begins to bolster a sense of superiority in our own mind, that twist didn't take place in Alastair.

Somehow the Fall fell differently on him.

And so, therefore, did the Light.

I remembered back to the evening when old friends had come to visit Mum and Dad, in shock and tearful apprehension over the news that their newborn baby girl had Down's syndrome. I thought about how my parents had stayed up late into the evening with this shaken couple listening to their fears and trying their best to answer their questions. I remembered how Alastair, returning home from an evening out, had heard voices in the sitting room and gone in to greet the guests. And how, on spying the carrycot with sleeping newborn, he had exclaimed, "Ahhh a baby!" and shot across the room to kneel beside her and, making the sign of the cross on her forehead, had said, "God bless you in the name of the Father and of the Son and of the Holy Spirit."

Ali was a vision of life lived out in the light, nowhere near the cover of a fig tree. He reached for the value in people that was beyond their posturing. Like when he was given his first camera and the developed photos were sent back and we saw the people Alastair noticed and thought worth photographing, each one an important, deliberate click of space on his film …

The postman leaning his bike against our hedge.

The postman waving and smiling as he rode off.

The refuse collector bow-shouldered under the weight of a bin, saluting at his photographer.

The refuse collectors hanging off their truck waving.

Mum, in her dressing gown, curled up in her favourite chair in the nest, before everyone else was up.

Me, asleep.

Rosalind, asleep.

Edward, the cat, curled up on the end of Rosalind's bed.

Dad sitting up in bed with cup of tea and Bible open on his lap.

The workmen shovelling cement in the middle of our road.

Eric, the elderly and infirm veteran from further along the street, resting on a garden wall.

The driver of a lorry leaning out of his cab with his thumb up.

Butterflies mating.

Alastair saw value that lay beyond status and appearances. But it didn't always work the other way around, it was an unfair trade-off. And here in front of the mirror I heard him count the cost. Feeling the sadness behind his desire to look more like me I wrapped my arms around his neck and leant my head onto his shoulder. I wished we who loved Ali could have been the only voices that really mattered. To have had the power to swat and bat away all accusations of abnormality from his consciousness, to have been able to instill in him the knowledge of the complete adoration and love that he inspired in us, despite all the infuriation he could often provoke.

I had watched Alastair go forward for healing at every healing service possible. Any time a preacher had asked from the stage where the person with a bad knee or slipped disc was, because God had told him He wanted to heal it, Ali would shoot up to the front ready to receive healing of Down's syndrome. But God never did tell any preacher man that He was minded to set someone free from that kind of disability. Maybe Ali eventually realized, in those moments spent waiting at the foot of the pulpit, that Down's syndrome wasn't on God's list of problems to be sorted. I, meanwhile, had always watched on, nervous that God might see Alastair's faith – which was acres larger than a mustard seed – and somehow heal him. But I was always glad when He didn't. I didn't want Alastair to be returned to us devoid of that extra chromosome, unrecognizable and incomplete. There was no version of Alastair that wasn't infused by Down's syndrome, just like there was no version of him that wasn't infused with our blend of English-Scottish-Scandinavian DNA.

Though I would happily have seen the Down's label scored from his medical records, I didn't want my brother to no longer be himself. The label might have had its uses in the early days, like a metronome setting a more appropriate tempo for Mum and Dad and their expectations. But beyond that it was useless. Alastair didn't need a diagnosis to help him index his capacities and gifts and the meaning his life would have. Down's syndrome was a word used by doctors and social workers, or by people who felt the need to make him feel that that was all he was. But Down's syndrome wasn't a definition Alastair needed; he was too busy living out the meaning of words like courage, determination, strength, enthusiasm and encouragement to be undermined by negative expectations.

Now that I realized how the label had become a taunt to Ali's mind I wondered about surgery once again. The accusations of being handicapped hurt him, not because it made him feel inferior, but because they made him feel he didn't belong, as if he wasn't really one of the rest of us. Would the loss of Alastair-ness be compensated for by him feeling 'normal' if, in some hypothetical Swiss medical technology laboratory, a way of removing that extra chromosome became possible? And would we let Ali make the decision to fix a problem that only existed as far as others made it a problem? Or would we realize that some things in life get broken when we try to fix them?

Where for most of us the snares set by others snag on the fabric of our ego, for Ali they cut into him, causing him to question his place and belonging and worth. There is no surgery for that: he had to live in the struggle and costliness and richness of that reality and we had to be with him in it. Looking at Alastair there it became clear to me that we had to help him inhabit himself so rootedly that the snares and snarls of others wouldn't pull him out of who he was. Maybe it was grace, a kind of protection, which kept Alastair, and those like him, from the bungling, mangling attempts of medical cures, and drew us to look in a different direction for wholeness?

And what about the offer of surgery that still lay open to me? Mr Harrison had been good to his word and kept the date in his diary. There were six weeks until that date and I looked ahead towards it, for the first time in several months. Here now, away from church and sermons about Abraham it began to look different. It seemed less like a temptation put there by God for me to proudly resist, and more like a gift sitting in the open hand of a God I'd not encountered for a very long time. A God who seemed more like a mother, an older sister looking at me the way I looked at Ali. Someone understanding, and compassionate, and kind. A presence, gently beckoning me to stop trying to be so perfect and together. To see that it was OK to let the leaves of self-righteous pride fall away because He had me covered already. A presence who wasn't planning how to smite me for taking the gift laid open to me, but who was giving me the choice and either way would find a way to make me whole, with or without the facial reconstruction.

This was freedom. Knowing that all was not lost … that I would not be lost, whatever decision I made.

* * *

When Dad had brought me home from university my doctor had talked to me about the need for anti-depressants. The idea did not appeal. It seemed like denial; cheating the reality that I was hurting.

So I tried hard to do better; I tried to pray the darkness away and tell my fear that it wasn't the Truth. I carried little cards in my pocket with Bible verses written out on them by Dad.

"For the Spirit that God has given us does not make us timid; instead, His Spirit fills us with power, love, and self-control."[1]

"Cast all your anxiety on Him because He cares for you."[2]

"The peace of God, which passes all understanding, will guard your hearts and minds in Christ Jesus."[3]

It was just like a monumental game of mind over matter that I called faith, and which was really my proud and desperate attempt to prove to God that I was deserving and good enough. I couldn't see that this was just another variant of suppression and denial.

But our soul knows its way home, and the truth cracks its way out between the fissures in our integrity somehow, and sooner or later it etches its insistent presence on the canvas of our bodies if it finds no other voice. Which is possibly why my throat had become such a battleground, constricting so tightly that the thought of solid food was unbearable. The relentless roiling of anxious dread in my tummy, an aching tremble in my limbs, my mind dark and hopeless: whatever Bible verses I was reciting they weren't doing the magic trick I expected of them.

Now, sitting in front of the doctor, explaining my reluctance to turn to pills, he told me, gently, that I was breaking under the strain. "Think of when someone breaks an arm," he suggested, "it gets put in a cast to protect it while it heals. For you it is the same, you need something to hold your mind still while you heal and become strong again. Imagine anti-depressants as that cast."

---

[1] 2 Timothy 1.7
[2] 1 Peter 5.7
[3] Philippians 4.7

I wanted to know myself as that; unbroken, strong, healed. There had been a summer, in 1992, when I had felt what that was like. Three fabulous weeks in which I headed out to Romania with 26 other teenagers to help build a church and run a children's summer camp in the Roma community. It was the first time in my teen years that my face didn't seem to be noticed. I was able to take an affectionate place in everyone else's banter and to be able to return it freely, not screwed up in shy angst over the irrelevance of my affections or unsure they would be welcomed. The vivacity of our post-exam high spirits and our excitement at the Transylvanian adventure ahead of us broiled these friendships, forging them in laughter, camaraderie and deep trust, sealing them for decades to come.

Several Etonians were on the trip, among them Bear Grylls, and, clearly happy to be free from an all-male environment for a little while, they lavished their grandiose flirtations upon the girls. *"Santa Joanna!"* Bear would drawl in exclamation, opening arms wide towards me, *"Quien en el mundo es más maravilloso que tu?"* It didn't matter that 50 seconds later he was mooning over Santa Victoria as she walked across his path with another pile of bricks. "No one, Bear! No one in the world is quite as wonderful!" I laughed back shyly over my shoulder.

Those weeks in Romania went way beyond just feeling included, merely on the receiving end of everyone's graces, patronized but still not really a person in my own way. The bliss of that trip was finding I was as lively, generous-spirited and ordinary as everyone else. For those weeks, I larked, I laughed, sang children's action songs to bewildered Romanian children and felt as if I was growing into new rooms; becoming an undiscovered version of myself.

That freedom, that unselfconsciousness to give of oneself without fear that you'll be rejected because your jawbone has grown a little too enthusiastically was surely the freedom that surgery would make possible. My mind skipped ahead of the doctor's words about anti-depressants to the thought of being un-cast from negative reactions and living unfurled from that small, tight place. It wasn't that the surgery was going to change who I was, it would just give a chance for me to come out of hiding. That was what I wanted.

14

About Face

Six weeks later I stood in front of the mirror in the hospital bathroom trying to fix the image before me in my mind, so that in years to come I would be able to remember what it was like to be here on this side of the knife, in this face.

Eleven hours later I was tucked up in morphined oblivion on the intensive care unit (ICU) I'd been to visit the day before. During my stay here I saw little but heard everything I needed to know: the arrival of my Mum and Rosalind, the scrape of their plastic chairs as they sat down by my bed, the scrape of one chair and the footsteps of one of them leaving.

Then the nurse's kind voice, "Would you like me to see if she's OK?"

She wasn't talking about me.

It was Rosalind who had left, unable to stomach the sight of me; ventilator in mouth, garish bruising across a swollen face that now, finally, deserved the nickname "Chipmunk", and two tubes sewn into my neck, draining blood into two bottles either side of me.

"Perhaps if you could … I think it's just shocked her a bit", Mum replied.

From the darkness I tried to heave my eyes open.

I saw the edge of the tape holding my nasal feeding tube in place and beyond it my Mum's arms and hands reaching across the sheets to hold my hand. Then sleep overcame me once more.

Into the disorienting tumble of delirium I plunged. Pumped with enough anaesthetic to last eleven hours, swiftly followed by morphine and antibiotics, despite repeated attempts to bring me round I only wanted to surrender to sleep. Mum and Dad called my name, holding up a Get Well card in front of my face, and I tried to follow the words but couldn't hold my eyes open long enough to catch who it was from.

Eventually, it was decided to let the pain wake me up and I was moved out of the ICU and into a side room on the ward. One by one the tubes were removed from my wrists, nose and arms, but I held onto my self-medicating morphine button, and the two bottles of blood remained on either side, my steady companions safely catching the blood away from my throat.

Shakily I tried to stand up for the first time, my legs trembling with doubt that my muscles would uphold me. My stomach was now concave, the loss of weight had become dangerous and my brand new hospital pyjamas hung from my bony hips. Despite the constant instruction to drink, the challenge was more bother than it was worth; my lips were swollen open and it required too much effort to keep the water from spilling back down my chin, and so I avoided the indignity of it. Mr Harrison didn't care for my laissez-faire attitude and we had our first altercation. Though I vigorously shook my head at him when he threatened to put the nasal gastric tube back down I knew that ultimately he would win the battle. And so each sip, each cup, each pint of water became my daily goal.

Then there were mirrors; the undeniable proof that what felt so alien about my own face indeed was. For a while I tried to avoid them, not wanting to see what this swollen facial bulk actually looked like. The emergence of my features was a long way down the road. Mr Harrison had told me that I would need another operation to build my chin and that it would be a year before the swelling would go down fully and my facial tissues and muscles would settle into their new shape. For now the days were for waiting and learning to sip water, prune juice or whatever else Mum and Dad could liquidize.

In those mute weeks I carried a clipboard around to make myself understood and, inhabiting a quiet place in the social whirl of visitors coming and going during the long, hot summer, I watched and listened in. Life lay ahead with a new kind of unpredict-ability. Who could tell if it was nursing that I wasn't suited to or whether it was just the fall-out from the bullying. I wasn't sure that I wanted to start again and find out. But sooner or later I would have to discover what life was going to be like now. What ground would it be built upon? Would this new, squarer jaw really be the foundation of a different existence? In moments of impatience I wanted to know what life now held for me. I wanted to know what I was going to look like. The only response was the reflection of a chubby, shortened face in the mirror with Hannibal Lecter-style caging across my teeth. Whatever life was going to be, I couldn't seize it yet. But the waiting left me with the question: who might I become once I had choices, once I began living in the spaciousness of a different life?

Beyond the scrapes with Mara at college or the arrival of poison-pen letters, I was nineteen and Rachel Humsley's words had caught up and sunk me. I had succumbed to her words as if falling prey to a curse: something whose magnitude I couldn't understand at the time, until I found myself living within its confines.

15

Undoing

I used to think of the words God spoke to Eve and Adam as a curse too. The Curse. The literal Mother of all Curses that would crack down, overshadow and jolt in all relationships, all desires, all labouring mothers and jaded toilers evermore. Except it wasn't. It turns out that for years I was just misreading it or being inattentive in Sunday school. Because when Adam and Eve are told to come out of their hiding-places in the bushes, where they had been cowering with shame and fright, it isn't them who are cursed: it's the serpent, the purveyor of illusions and author of their doubts.

When God eventually turns to Eve, it's different. He just tells her how it is going to be now.

"I will greatly increase your pains in childbearing;
with pain you will give birth to children."

But even though it's not an actual curse, I've still struggled with this passage. Because it's so deliberate. It may not have strictly been a curse, but try telling that to a woman overdosing on gas and air as she pushes out a 10-pound baby.

And it won't stop there. God goes on with something ambiguous about her still desiring her husband, and then something that isn't hazy at all; He says that her husband will rule over her.

They feel so broken, unable to belong here any longer. They have to leave, and remove their trailing messes with them.

Only they are not broken, because that would have been the end. Instead this departure becomes the start of a different journey in which they will make their way, still bearing memories of beauty, of peace and trust, and learn to re-member love.

At first it doesn't feel that hopeful for Eve. She is still puzzling over that line about desiring her husband and the clanging adjunct that he's going to rule over her. Trying to figure out what this actually means.

I could tell her what it would mean, any woman could. Any one of us could find our own starting-point where we experience that inequality, even if we don't actually name it.

Like the teenage girl who is afraid of boys, because they tell her she's ugly. Who feels annoyed that she can't shrug it off and not mind because they're clearly not nice people. Who wishes she had the kind of self-possession not to care what anyone thinks of her looks, but all the time can't help wishing that they didn't feel like that about her so that she could dare to hope that one of them might one day like her and want to be with her. So it might not have been an actual curse, but being unpretty at nineteen felt hopeless.

That's the first thing: seeing where we feel cursed or trapped. Then waking up and seeing the meaning we attach to our suffering. Watching how we let it persuade us that we will be left alone, that our longing for connection is futile or, perhaps, that we don't deserve to hope for something really good. We might then begin to notice how we collude with these fearful conclusions and settle into uneven ways of relating to others. Or we might see how we try with all our might to disprove the calculations we've made about the world, and how we single-handedly try to rearrange reality with exhausting determination, doing all we can to avoid the future we fear.

Because inequality is a reality within which we find ourselves living, in one way or another. Sometimes it can seem to be a curse, but perhaps it's also a reminder that we're not yet Home, not yet whole, and that the fractures of the Fall aren't for us alone to mend.

That's the paradox: that God allows us to be tripped up so that we remember we were never made to be alone and that we are not expected to put things right by ourselves.

And so, having been tripped up by our efforts to put on a good show, we come to see that they're not where freedom and redemption lie. Maybe we come to see the twisted truths about women and men as something more like an invitation; something that reminds us that, even though it's not down to us to put things right, we're welcome to join in with God's re-membering of love, beauty, and truth in the world.

And we begin perhaps to feel the untangling of the fig leaves and branches behind which we've tried to hide, and to sense the presence of someone who says "*It's OK, you don't need to pretend.*" Who gently, leaf by leaf, helps us to let go of our disguises and our attempts at independence and instead clothes us warmly with Love.

Those words God spoke to Eve are heard by each of us in our own particular way. They are words that at first seem to convict and imprison. But somehow they can become the words that begin to set us free.

16

Hot Worship Leaders and Godly Wives

Out from behind the swollen weld of wired jaws and clamped mouth this new face slowly began to emerge. A sheet of paper arrived in the post from a fashion designer friend, Harris. Sketched across it were a series of portraits offering various possibilities for styling my wired face.

The Frankenstein bolt

The astronaut

The scaffold lips

The zoo cage

The crane mouth

The naughty brother version complete with electrodes attached to a plug …

Rosalind and I pored over it, laughing and, instinctively, my hand shot up to my mouth to cover it. Only something was different. The familiar bump of my palm against my teeth didn't happen. My fingers pushed gently against my face to trace this new absence. But all I could feel was the almost-closed poise of my lips protecting my jaw from my searching fingers. *It's tucked away in here*, they seemed to retort, *you have no business doing our job for us now*. That was it, I no longer needed to cover up my laughter and smiles and I began to resist the automatic dash of my hand up to my face.

The need for a scissor-holding chaperone to accompany me in case of sudden vomiting and choking hazards came to an end when, after two months, Mr Harrison cut the wires and told me I could go forth and eat. The pizza I'd been dreaming of was still a milestone or two away but, tentatively experimenting with spoonfuls of mashed potato and baked beans, I felt my way around this new mouth. There was giddy disbelief at the ease with which I could now close my mouth and eat. The curve of my stomach and the etch of my ribcage against my bare back began to give way to soft, fleshy weight and, starting each day with a class of ballet, my weak, toneless body began to fill out once again. I'd felt little more than a shuffling skeleton, from which my clothes had gaped and hung all summer, but by the autumn I began to find my stride. The hair, reaching down towards my waist in a mousy tumble, brushed down to hide my embarrassing profile, was no longer needed. And as is so often the case with women marking the beginning of a new season of life, I let my hair tell the story, cutting it into a neat bob that curled back behind my ears. I was coming out of hiding.

It was time to find a new church too. I was living with my parents indefinitely and I didn't want to return to the church I'd grown up in, so I looked for a congregation to become part of as my own person, not as John and Didi's daughter. Whatever estrangement I felt from God, I was still at home with Christians; they were my family, my people whose language I spoke. The kindness and purpose with which people at Emmanuel Church made their way in the world had never stopped providing me with a place to belong and the belief that there was a task for me also. They had covered every minute of unconsciousness throughout those eleven hours of surgery with their prayers. They were my home base, the people with whom I'd grown and prayed and holidayed. So, without cutting any ties with my Emmanuel family, I sought to find my place among a new group of Christians.

I found a church in another town. My grandparents had taken me there once, and it seemed perfect. Always suspicious of a church full of only one age group, this one immediately appealed with its packed congregation spanning children to pensioners, and most crucially, its plentiful students and twenty-somethings. Throughout the opening blare of praise and worship people sang and danced, and I stood, studying the words of the unfamiliar songs, trying to memorize the words and tune so that I too could sing with my eyes shut and my arms uplifted in praise of God.

God. Of course it was all about God. Except God was the awkward factor in the midst of this new foray. For the first few weeks I didn't notice the growing unease, the vague return of that churning worry as I left after coffee. There was too much to do. Morning church led into prayer ministry and coffee. Then there was an open house invitation to all the young adults where proper grown-ups welcomed us into their lovely homes and fed us and allowed us to sprawl all over their sitting rooms, chatting and eating, until we felt the need to walk it all off in the fresh air before heading back to the evening celebration service. Sundays were brilliant now. Especially the Sunday where, as the pastor stood welcoming us, my eyes dropped down to the guy in the band, perched behind him, and met his eyes and saw his slow, shy smile. I stared at him for a moment, unused to being gazed at without disdain or smirking derision. But there was no smirk, just a flittering tremor in my stomach.

He was one of the assistant pastors, the kind of promising young man that the elders were training to become a preacher man. Good looking, a cool, worship-band guitarist, mauled by adoring children

during coffee time and more subtly surrounded by the adulation
of the students during open home lunches, Rich was going places
with God and every single girl wanted to go with him. Which made
concentrating on God during worship pretty tricky, when you
knew that your passion for God could be easily surveyed by Rich
as he stood looking out at the congregation, leading us deeper into
worship.

Would I be spiritual enough for him? I worried the next Sunday
and I stretched up both arms, closed my uplifted eyes and sang a
little more enthusiastically just to show him I was. It was part of
the alternative mating ritual that belongs to a charismatic Christian
subculture. Some rules were the same in or out of church: boys in
the band definitely get the girls and he was a worship leader pin-up.
So when Rich approached me over coffee a few Sundays later to see
if I was coming on a walk later that afternoon I decided I definitely
would.

Lunch that day was at the home of one of the elders, Cliff, and
his wife, Janet, and rumour was it was going to be good. From my
Sunday to Sunday views of Janet I suspected the rumours were
right. Ruffled blouses articulating her buttoned modesty, three sons
regularly turned out in matching home-made waistcoats, Cliff's
leadership duly supported by her organization of the women's
Bible study and prayer meeting, Janet seemed to have stepped
straight out of Proverbs 31 and into the twentieth century with her
version of wifely perfection; her cooking was bound to be a treat.
Shuffling out of our shoes we padded into their wide, neat sitting
room, immediately violating its magnolia hues with our mishmash
of studenty attire. Rich grabbed a pile of cushions – home-made
chintz covers to match the home-made curtains – and stacked them
up behind his head and stretched out across the floor. It was too
much of an invitation to the boys, the youngest of whom spotted

the opportunity to launch off the back of the armchair in a dive aimed at Rich's chest. "Aaron, would you come here please." Janet recalled her son, diverting him firmly towards a suitably hospitable job taking drinks orders from us all.

Rich leaned up on his elbows, seizing an audience as we settled into armchairs and sofas, and asked what we thought of Justin's sermon that morning. Polite murmurs of "It was good" rippled among the group until Justin himself strode towards us and Rich tilted his chin towards him, "I'm just taking the temperature following your sermon, Jus!"

"So what were my three points then?"

Justin nudged Rich to move his legs and make room on the floor. I furiously scanned my mental notes on Titus Chapter 3 from the morning's service but it was the previous week's sermon on Titus Chapter 2 that was still playing on my mind.

Sara and Lois had a brave go at piecing together the first and second points while Justin smiled at them, almost hiding his weary frustration that his hours of sermon crafting had already dissipated in the melee of social distractions.

He turned to me, "Joanna! What was the third point?"

I could feel Rich's eyes on me, and his wry smile as he bit gently on his lower lip, watching and waiting.

"Your final point was about living full of the Holy Spirit … so that we begin to put our focus and energy into things that God is about in the world."

"And how do we stay in tune?"

"Well … by prayer, fellowship, reading the Bible, remembering that it's not our own goodness so we keep returning to God's goodness to work through us."

"Good!" He was about to move on, but before he could I blurted my irritation.

"But then last week was all about behaving as good Christians. All the older women in the church teaching the younger women how to behave correctly … and basically be good housewives!"

The other girls on the sofa watched quietly to see where this was going to go.

"Yes, it also told the men to be self-controlled and sincere and gracious in their teaching."

"I know, it's just that on the one hand you're teaching us to be filled with the Spirit which sounds full of possibility … being alive to God so that we can do his work in the world, but on the other hand we are just given a template of a good Christian girl – or man – to emulate. It seems a little …"

Janet swept into the room to invite the girls to go and get their food from the kitchen first.

"… contrived", I finished, but the word didn't reach far enough; it didn't name the growing frustration I was feeling.

"Janet, Joanna was just commenting on last week's sermon and the call to women to live a holy life."

I stood up to follow the others out but Janet looked at me, waiting, "Yes, indeed!", she nodded. I tried again, "It's not the holy life thing that I'm on about … it's the holy life of domesticity while men are almost automatically told to be leaders."

"Well let me just get everyone sorted out and we can have a talk about that over lunch."

I had been dismissed to the girls' class, and suddenly the appetizing spread of Thai chicken curry felt as if it came at an uncomfortable price. It also meant that I wasn't going to get to hang out with Rich during the lunch. I felt as though I needed to apologize to the other girls for getting their lunch hijacked by a seminar on wifeliness but they were more than happy to have Janet come and sit with them in the conservatory where the all-female gathering put off any male disturbance.

If I was worried I would have to give an account of my hesitation about gender roles in the Kingdom of God, Janet's unflinching launch into an explanation of women's civilizing nature soon disabused me. I kept my eyes on the plate of food in my hand while she seized this moment to be the older, wiser woman so applauded in St Paul's letter to Titus.

"… and as women we are clearly called to complement our husbands by submitting to them, by supporting them in the Lord's work and doing this with a gentle, beautiful spirit. That's where people go so wrong in thinking beauty is all about outward appearance and good looks: it's not! It's the unfading beauty of our feminine spirit that we need to cultivate because that is the strength that we offer to our husbands."

Lois leaned her head to the side, combining a smile with a gentle frown even St Paul couldn't find fault with. "But we still need to attract a man in the first place and men like to be with beautiful-looking women … I mean, I know it's not everything but I want my husband to find me beautiful."

"And he will, the man God has for you will see your beauty shine through. You don't need to worry about being beautiful because on your wedding night you will be the most glorious woman in the world to him."

I looked up at Janet to see if this line had been delivered with any spark of jollity but she was unsmiling and unwilling to let even a brief hiatus divert the conversation from her message.

"When Cliff and I were engaged we went to a friend's house-party and our hosts put us in bedrooms next to each other. It was the most foolish thing. They should have put us in rooms at opposite ends of the house. *Opposite* ends!"

She swept her arm vigorously out to the side to indicate just how far apart they ought to have been housed.

"But it was my purity and strength that got us through that – I think Cliff would have been too tempted by opportunity and desire. We came through that weekend without sin because God showed me that I had to be strong for both of us."

"So that's how women complement men? By keeping them from being their own worst enemy?"

"Yeah, so don't try and be too attractive; you'll just lead men into sin!" Laura joked.

"It's true!" Janet pounced. "If we are to enable men to be the leaders, the holy men of God that they are called to be, then we have a vital task in watching our own behaviour and maintaining the purity of our own hearts so that we don't cause them to sin."

"So you didn't sin before you were married then?" Lois asked, her bluntness pushing at the subject that was really of interest to her.

"Cliff and I were virgins when we got married."

There it was, the benchmark of a young adult's walk with the Lord: that you had pledged to keep sex until you were married and could give it as an unblemished gift to your husband or wife. Virginity was where the purity and wholeness of our soul was crystallized, safely out of the way, between our legs, where it wouldn't be disturbed or disturb anyone else until The Right Time.

At camp when I was seventeen an American preacher man had called all the single people up to the front of the Severn Barn where he led us in a prayer to commit to staying celibate until our wedding night. After we'd prayed this promise he told us to open our eyes and look around and see who was available. "Take a look! You want to get married? Well look at all these other singles with a heart after God like your own." Maybe that bit of the scenario had gone down better in the States, because in a crowd of Brits the invitation to look around at who was available made us take an awkward sidelong glance and then drop our reddened faces downwards hoping for the spectacle to be over soon.

It didn't surprise me that this was Janet's answer: that her interpretation of the word sin merely equated with sex; we each knew that the only sin that really counted was sexual. But I thought then about my attempt to get Rich to think I was holy. What about that kind of sin? The things that we do to portray ourselves as something we're not. I remembered Sara's words to me weeks before: that not going to bed with a man was the quickest way to get him up the aisle. Her eyes had twinkled with knowing power as she let me into the secret. But when I'd asked her if she was more concerned with just getting a man up the aisle than being with the right man at the altar, she'd shrugged me off. "Of course it will be the right man."

Where were all the sermons teaching us how to speak the truth in relationships instead of hiding behind phrases about it "being right" or "not God's will"? Where was the rigorous teaching helping us to see better when a partner is manipulating you … or when we were manipulating them? The great intricacies of emotional and spiritual ties that lace their way through our encounters with each other, even when we weren't physically touching, were never talked about. They weren't acknowledged, because apparently those places weren't where sin took root. So we were never taught how to get to know someone and work out whether marriage was a good idea. As long as you could make it to your wedding day, virginity intact, then you were whole and pure and blessed.

"So was it wonderful?" Lois asked, slightly dreamily.

"It really isn't like the films, girls." Janet's jaw jutted forward as she shut her mouth and looked at each of us, making sure we were absorbing the gravity of this news.

"The next morning I went to the loo and there was a rush of blood ... just a great rush."

"Eurgh!"

"Owwwww."

I put my hands up to my face, as uncomfortable with being told this information as I was with the information itself.

"Seriously?"

"Absolutely, it was quite painful. I came down to breakfast unable to walk properly. So there were a few sympathetic smiles from other women at the hotel."

Her moral exposition ceased for a moment. She took a few mouthfuls of curry, watching with satisfaction as we absorbed these fearful sexual realities.

"But why do women have one night stands then?" Grace puzzled, "I mean if it's so painful ..."

"Eugh! I know ..."

"That's awful, there's no way I'm going to have sex before I get married. No way!"

Janet let the buzz of concern and anxiety anchor us firmly on the side of abstinence before announcing that she needed to go and see to pudding. We sat there grimacing before Sara tried to smooth things over, "At least when we get married we'll be with someone we love. We don't really need to be worried when it's the man God has chosen for us to marry."

There it was again, the salve that we applied to every problem: if it's the right person, the person God's chosen, then everything will be OK.

I wondered if Rich was The Right Person for me. I leaned over my shoulder to look back into the sitting room at what the rest of them were doing. Tucking into puddings, Rich and his brother were engrossed in conversation with Cliff, no doubt talking about strategies and leadership opportunities and all the other manly stuff that they got to do. At least I would have a chance to talk to him later if we went for a walk, or afterwards at the youth workers' meeting.

17

At Home in a Stable

The church ran training for people who wanted to become street youth pastors and I had volunteered enthusiastically – even before I knew that Rich was involved. On Friday and Saturday evenings teams would go out into the small towns where little was going on for teenagers, and provide a safe presence in streets and parks decorated by used syringes and strewn bottles. I was partnered with Geoff, a retired man of fathomless patience and gentleness, and an easy readiness to laugh. Out on the streets we strolled our route and chatted to the kids we met, who were happy to have some attention, an audience who might care what destruction they were prepared to kick up.

Joe was one of the young people we met and, at seventeen, was one of the oldest teens we met on our evening rounds of the park, the cemetery, the churchyard and the car park outside the newsagent. He was a punk, his hair brightly dyed a different colour each week, and had clear blue eyes that spun round and round from all the speed he was taking. Joe was the eldest of three children and, having encountered the reckless mischief of his young brother and sister, seemed to be a gentler soul. Yet his relationship with his parents had broken down and now he was squatting or bunking down in stables, eating barely anything, except ice-cream.

Geoff and I began to look forward to seeing Joe and spending some of the evening with him and his friends, Leon and James. They wanted to know why we bothered spending our Friday and Saturday nights in this amble around the town, and their scoffing laughter at our reasons belied their relief at being taken seriously by some adults.

"So you gonna keep doing this then? This street work?" Leon asked, laughing as he caught Joe's eye.

"Yes, as long as there are kids out here running around drinking and taking drugs we will", Geoff replied.

"What about in the winter?"

"Well we'll probably open up the church and provide a place for you to come and keep warm and have some hot drinks", I reassured.

"Ahhh, I'll probably get struck down if I go in your church …" Joe smiled, plunging his hands into the pockets of his trousers. He looked down at his feet and rocked back on his heels.

"Joe, I'll bring the hot chocolate out to you if you're that scared!"

"You never know what's gonna happen if you step on God's turf." Leon shook his head, his smile broadening across his face while his lips pursed the remaining stub of his smoldering roll-up.

"I think you'd find there was a very warm welcome if you ever decided to come to church."

And of course they would have done. That was what we were praying for. Every Friday and Saturday as we met in the church to commit the coming evening into God's hands, naming each young person before Him, asking for His protection and blessing upon them. Going out to them was just part of the whole picture. We would go out and let them know that they mattered; but it was extending an invitation to them to join us in church that completed the circle.

"*And Lord, we just pray for your blessing upon each of those young people we meet tonight … fill us with your Holy Spirit that your light would shine upon them and reveal your love to each of them.*"

"*We pray for you to open up opportunities for good conversations and give us your wisdom as we respond to their questions and searching …*"

"*Yes Lord, bless them and bring them to know your love for them and to receive you in their hearts.*"

One by one we sought to put into words what we longed for God to do. We wanted His blessing, we wanted the revelation of His love, and we wanted to see the transformation of lives, we wanted spiritual revival. And in each of our minds we held a picture of what that would look like. It had already begun: the arrival of young men like Pete and Matthew who had started regularly attending church and open home lunches. The hardships with which life had punched them were evident in physical flares of anger, or in the curses tattooed across hand and neck, in the prayer ministry they sought from their male mentors and their spats of anger when the possibility of a trustworthy father figure became too frightening. Over the months we had seen these men commit their lives to God, and swear words give way to hallelujahs as they became Christians, like us.

That's what revival meant: church services overflowing. People praising, praying, being healed. Prayer ministry where people fell down, slain in the Spirit, overpowered by the presence of God so that they could no longer stand up. Lives less ordinary, supernaturally altered. Of course it was what I wanted too, the touch of God filling the craterous space that my nursing career had left. Week after week, with eyes squeezed shut, the familiar prayers rained down over me, delivered by the voices of conviction belonging to the men at the front.

I, too, knew how to string the right buzzwords together to make prayers like that. My conversations with Christians were mingled with bilingual fluency, incorporating clichés about faith and reaching easy conclusions about the sovereignty of God's control in all situations. Talk of God's love spilt easily into my prayers and chatter. And yet the anxious knot tugged in my stomach and unsettled my worship. I heard myself spouting words of adoration towards God but they seemed to do nothing more than hang like fridge magnets, suspended silently, going nowhere. Whichever way I rearranged them they stayed before me, empty of meaning. In the happy-clappy bubble of this church I had willingly regurgitated countless prayers and praises, putting myself out there as the woman of God I had been brought up to be. Now the words were beginning to stick in my mouth.

When Justin exhorted us to all stand up and shout our praises to God simultaneously, I tried and failed, too distracted by the bellowing prayers of those around me to conjure up any authentic praise of my own. The torrential jargon of our worship and our conversations began to seem like whitewash over life and I wanted to scratch away at it, to look and examine what truth lay beneath it.

I wanted to chip away at all the assumptions about our lives as Christians, and as men and women of God. Why was it that God only seemed to show up powerfully in *our* charismatic evangelical churches? We were so hung up on the signs of the Spirit that we remained blind to the reality of God's flourishing in other traditions. We discredited Roman Catholic and Anglican churches as merely *religious*: places of empty ritual where churchgoers weren't on fire for God. We didn't even discuss the possibility that the energy of God pulsed through the entire world, flourishing in all the dark places we called secular. Where was our recognition and delight in God's aliveness beyond our own careful constructions of the holy? And so we denied the reach of the very God we claimed to want to know so deeply.

I wanted to question these men who decreed from the pulpit and these women who coaxed us through their ladies' Bible studies. Why does simply being a man legitimate you as a preacher? Why does gentleness legitimate you as a woman of God? Why am I too afraid to ask these questions for fear of being seen as difficult and unruly, instead of teachable and gentle? And how is it that being a woman who bears God's image has been derailed and reduced to impersonating the maternal aspirations and dress sense of middle-class women in church?

18

Fish Out of Water

According to an urban parable I once heard these ways of thinking, these views that we hold, can be like the water in which a fish swims. If anybody ever asked us what the water was like we wouldn't know what they were talking about. A fish doesn't see the water it's swimming in; it lives and breathes it. Like fish, we swim around in all sorts of murkiness, circling through the same old patterns of thinking, relishing prejudices that are so familiar to us we no longer see what a comfort they've become, recycling behaviours that are so rehearsed we barely hear ourselves saying the lines any more. We can live and move and have our being in these things and never properly see or hear them.

Only when something happens, something that grabs us and takes us out of our normality, can we see it for the first time. And then we have a chance to see that we can choose to inhale and feed off different things. But mostly we don't freely reject our obsolete ways and thinking; to do so would feel almost deathly. These attitudes and patterns have to be prised from our clutches so that there is distance enough to observe them, so we can see that we are not those things and that we can approach life differently. Usually it's through something unpleasant, something we name as suffering. But without it we tend not to discover that the things we thought were holding us and protecting us were actually things that were keeping us small and stunted and hidden; like my misshapen beliefs about God.

Operating in a subculture where I expected to see signs and wonders meant that, if I wasn't experiencing any of the supernatural action, I would be reduced to the role of onlooker: a mere spectator, watching God's favour poured out upon others while I remained unchosen. So I couldn't let my zeal wane, I just kept praising. And now I was tired. My uplifted arms seemed to do little more than uphold the image of me as holy, prayerful, good. If that was the deal I had going on with the Almighty I was ready to bow out. It wasn't enough any longer to expend my energy proving to myself and others it was true. I wanted to live truthfully.

Unfearfully. Messily if I had to.

I knew I was outgrowing it; these superficial confines of our kind of Christianity. The language we used, the clothes we wore, the roles we could play; I no longer wanted to squeeze myself into their narrow parameters.

But it was during a sermon that Cliff preached that I suddenly saw, like a fish being held above the water, what beliefs I'd been swimming in. He was preaching about the return of the prodigal son and he roved about with the microphone making eye contact with us as he spoke about the Lost out there beyond the church who needed to be invited in to meet Jesus.

"They are the ones who need to come home and it's clear to us as a leadership team, and many of you too, that God is moving here among us; preparing us to welcome them home to the Father. It has already begun … and people, we need to be ready, prepared to show them this love of God that they so badly need."

I looked down at my Bible resting on my lap. I followed the story, it was titled 'The Lost Son' in my Bible. But as I read on I got to the bit about the elder son: the son who had never been bad and run away from home, the son who had not demanded and then squandered his inheritance. The son who had worked hard to be good and everything he ought to be. The son who in sinking disappointment and seething resentment turns on his father and asks, "Where's the party and fatted calf in *my* honour?"

There I was on the page. I had been watching for years as the Lost were returned and restored, celebrated and loved, and all the time I hadn't been able to understand why I couldn't speak of God's love in the way that these prodigals could. Fast-tracked through a childhood of systematic indoctrination at camps and house parties and seminars and Sunday school, the moment of being filled with wonder at God's love had passed too quickly. Once we'd made our prayers of commitment we were moved on to new levels: learning the scriptures, evangelizing, upholding morality, learning to portray ourselves as a particular brand of Christian. Surrounded by our Christian role models, we were shaped into their mould; we imitated goodness, and came to believe we had a monopoly on it.

We listened to the good news about the Father who received back his prodigal younger son with great rejoicing. But for us who had been brought up to be elder brothers, it seemed as though they – the love, the fatted calf, the warm welcome – didn't belong to us. I didn't believe in that Father God because I'd not encountered that God; I'd never wandered off and wound up eating pigs' leftovers and then returned to find that incredible home-coming.

My need to be good really came down to the terror of needing forgiveness. I was an elder brother working so hard not to give God something to hold over me. And now I was stuck, clutching onto the false self I'd been manufacturing all these years. Too tired to hold on any longer, I wondered what would happen when it all fell to pieces.

19

Napkins, Nails and Piercings

It's great when churches welcome the lost into its services, but it's the exclusivity of the after-show party which becomes the test of authentic acceptance. When homes, Sunday lunches and parties open up for outsiders to cross the threshold and become insiders. Laura and Matthew were the first to banish any question of whether the love for newcomers was authentic. She, the petite, middle-class flute teacher from Berkshire, and he, the protective giant by her side, scarred and limping with wounds carried over from a previous life; they were inseparable. I didn't want to taint their happiness with nosy questions about whether they were together romantically and I hoped nobody else did either. That kind of interference, especially from church leaders, could tear at a friendship like impatient fingers pulling at the closed petals of a rosebud, demanding to know what it will look like and be. So I watched them, secretly triumphant that their togetherness bore witness to something genuine happening to us at church. It wasn't all about the Christians benevolently giving and the poor and vulnerable gladly receiving. We could be vulnerable too – God might be changing the elder brothers as much as the prodigals.

When Joe began turning up to church more frequently on Sunday mornings it was probably because of the free cups of tea, or shelter from the rain, more than the sermons. It didn't matter why; everyone smiled at us sitting together and celebrated his progress. There he was, the latest prodigal to return. As Geoff and I spent more time with him and the others on Friday and Saturday evenings it became easier to talk without the forced mantle of holiness I felt compelled to display at church. I liked them and would have been happy just to chat with them. But they knew that we were there to evangelize and so they asked searching questions without any prompt from me.

"All that stuff he was talking about on Sunday, it's really going to happen, isn't it?" Joe was sitting on a swing, twisting to the side as he pushed his foot against the post. I was seated on the other swing and I looked at him, turned slightly away from me, trying to follow what he was talking about.

"Which man on Sunday?"

"The one giving the talk, all that stuff he was saying about hell and the apocalypse."

"He was talking about Revelation, it's a really tricky book to understand …" I took a deep breath, steeling myself for where this conversation might demand we go.

"But it's really gonna happen, isn't it?"

"Joe, I don't know exactly what's going to happen … Or what it will look like. Those things he was talking about are one man's vision … It's really hard to know exactly what he was seeing."

Joe walked the swing backwards and stood poised, ready to let himself sail through the air. But he didn't move, he stayed looking ahead, his clear blue eyes steady for once.

"What do you think is going to happen?"

"Well, the bit about how God is going to make his home with people, and there will be no more crying, or pain, or death, that makes sense … I think God knows that that's what we're trying to find ultimately. So I'm not sure about what the apocalypse will actually be, but it seems that the bit God is aiming for is to bring us all home. To restore us and make us whole."

He was looking at me and I could see he was troubled. I hadn't anticipated that the theological things spoken at church would affect him so much. I tried to prompt him:

"Which bit is bothering you most?"

I knew which bit was bothering me: it would be trying to explain all the implications of Christ's sacrificial death on the cross, in a way that would have some kind of meaning to the dispossessed punk on the swing beside me. All those teen house-parties spent learning how to lead someone to Christ, with diagrams about penal substitution on the back of a napkin; what a misspent youth.

"I don't wanna be left out … I mean if it's really gonna happen."

I hesitated, wondering at which point to begin my worn tirade of evangelistic patter.

"But does it mean I gotta go to church all the time and stuff?"

I looked across to the children's roundabout on which James and Leon were slowly revolving as they chatted to Geoff standing next to it. If anyone else was here listening I would be giving Joe The Right Answer, telling him how he had to come to church because that is where he could worship God and find fellowship. I would push away the doubts I had about him coming to church, and ignore my worries about how being absorbed into a community of beige and navy, middle-class Christians might endanger his colour and his soul. I would overlook the fear I had of him being whitewashed, body, mind and soul, should he succumb to the very nice, respectable peer pressure of a congregation who were praying for him to be saved. I didn't want him to become one of us with our hallelujahs and frothy fervour. Joe was OK with his luminous soul and hair and the chains that lightly clacked as they swung between his ears and belt and belly button. He just wanted to find his way Home. And in those moments I wanted to scoop him up and piggyback him to the gates of heaven myself – "*He's with me!*"

"Joe, you don't have to come but you know that you're welcome whenever you do … but it's not a price you have to pay. Geoff and I won't stop coming to see you here if you did decide not to come to church …"

"But what about God?"

"He's here too. He knows your heart … what you've been through. He cares that you've got no home right now … you matter to God not just when you die but in what's happening to you right now."

The technicalities of Christological explanations fell away. What was done on that cross all those centuries ago was done. Joe didn't need the theological disseminations, or yet another sinner's prayer offered for him to repeat; he needed love to break into the bleakness and turmoil of his existence.

"You matter to me, and to Geoff too … and, I don't know them but I'm sure your parents feel dreadful about what's happened between you."

"You think me and God could be OK?"

"Yes I do Joe … I think that's what God wants and if that's what you want too, then yes …"

20

Saved through Childbirth

The questions Joe asked me, and the answers I gave him, stayed with me for days. In them I heard echoes of my own daring hopes: that God and I could be OK, that I might find a way home to God away from this church I'd not yet escaped. I wanted to know who … if … God was, away from all this.

Only I couldn't yet see any signs that pointed to God – Out There. The idea of finding somewhere to go with all my questions was forming without any obvious answer. Until two days later, when Dad told me he'd been praying for me, and the idea of theological college popped into his mind. It may not have been the world beyond that I was expecting; I knew that theological colleges were places where people trained to be vicars. But I also knew how extraordinary it was that the Almighty might have whispered this suggestion to my father; a man who didn't believe in women's ordination, or subjecting one's grasp of The Truth to the intellectual shakedown that theological studies would cause.

I wrote off to some nearby theological colleges and excitedly read the syllabus lists before passing them onto Cliff and Justin along with a request for some sponsorship. It was Cliff who called me in for a meeting to discuss it and he sat opposite me fanning the prospectuses out in front of him with a bemused expression on his face. "Look Joanna, have you prayed about this?"

That was code for *we don't think this is right for you but we would rather not tell you that to your face.* In fact, I hadn't specifically sat with hands folded, eyes closed and run through the reasons why I wanted to do this, then bolted on an Amen. I hadn't needed to. The sight of modules on pastoral care; Old and New Testament studies; psychology and spirituality of healing; poetry and theology; The Gospel of John; and ancient Hebrew had thrilled me with an excitement that nursing never had. This was exactly what I wanted to study.

Cliff was flicking through the papers as he continued.

"These courses are a lot of money, and really … I just don't think we can justify spending £500 so that you can go and do a training course."

"But look at the subjects they teach; there's mission, discipleship, New Testament and Old Testament studies … how is that not going to be worthwhile?"

He reddened and shifted his leg over his other knee.

"What would you be training for? Really, Joanna, you don't need Hebrew and Greek to fulfill God's call on your life."

"I do if I'm going to understand the Bible properly."

He knew where I was taking this. If the answer was no, I wanted him to admit the reason to me.

"You can get that kind of teaching here at church."

"But I can't get that kind of serious training at church."

He took a breath and leaned back in his chair. "Joanna, what do you need to be trained for? It's only pastors that require this kind of training course." He waved the wadge of papers down onto his knee with a slap.

"I think it's important for anyone wanting to deepen their questions and understanding about the Bible."

"That may be so but we simply can't put that kind of money into funding you when you're not going to be a pastor."

I didn't want to be a pastor, but I did believe that I had to make that decision and not have it assumed for me by church elders on account of my gender.

"I ... "

"Joanna look, you are going to make a wonderful wife and mother one day, you have a great vocation ahead. All these courses look interesting now but they won't serve you well as a wife and mother in the long term."

I had never actually heard someone in the twentieth century and on this side of the Atlantic own St Paul's line about women being saved through childbirth, but it crossed my mind that this was what he was getting at.

"Are you saying that women are saved by having children?"

We were both suspended in a hiatus of disbelief; I that he believed this and he that I was going to make him say it out loud.

"Well, it's not that women are saved by having children but that through that experience they are saved."

"I don't know what you mean."

I wasn't being facetious; it just made absolutely no sense.

"Well, through giving birth they are saved and know God's mercy ..." It seemed that this was the only time Cliff had ever had to justify this part of St Paul's writings.

"and God saves them ..."

At this point I was absolutely sure that there was nothing better I could do with my life than go and get some proper theological education.

"Cliff, that sounds really alarming. Are you saying that women's vocation as mothers is where they find salvation? What about women who can't have children? I don't particularly want to have children; where does that leave me? You teach that we have to marry a Christian man but everyone knows there aren't enough Christian men in the church to go round so what about all the leftover women? Unmarried and not quite saved!"

"Joanna, Joanna …", he held up his hands to slow the roll of indignation and quieten the accusatory tone that had crept into my voice.

"We know that we need to address the issue of getting men into church …"

"That in no way addresses the underlying theology you hold …"

I was about to lose it; a lifetime of unchallenged dogma curdled, ready to be spewed out, but I didn't have a close enough relationship with Cliff to hurl that kind of mess on him – no matter how much I felt he deserved it. The money, the sponsorship didn't matter, I would find a way to put myself through theological college, but I did need a reference from my church leaders.

"Look, I don't mind if you don't feel able to give me any money. But I need you to write a reference, will you do that?"

"Yes we will."

I suspected it would be the kind of promising reference that employers write when they desperately want to get rid of an employee.

"Thank you … I appreciate you giving me your blessing …"

"Ahhhh, Joanna, hold on … I didn't say you had our blessing."

Maybe I should have hurled on him after all. Instead I took it home, where Dad was making a cup of tea to take out to the garden. I told him how the conversation with Cliff had gone, and without taking his usual place on the side of the church leadership Dad put his fists on his hips and listened, making grim-sounding "hrrrmmm" noises.

"Seriously ... he actually said women were saved through childbirth ... Does he mean Christ's death and resurrection wasn't quite enough to cover women? Am I just waiting to get married and give birth before I'm truly initiated and saved? It's seems that all these preacher men use the Bible to dictate what women are meant to be like ... They say that following Christ is supposed to be about integrity and freedom but it pretty much comes down to persuading girls to be nice, virginal, teetotal and never swear ... and then we're supposed to go and sell that to the world!"

Dad chewed the corner of his lip and looked thoughtfully out towards the garden.

"It's not freedom, it's not the Gospel, it's just rules ... and come on, did I look like I was in any danger of fornicating at the age of fifteen when I was told not to be like a dress that gets tried on lots but nobody wants to buy? Did I?!"

I paused to draw breath and saw his eyes close slowly at the memory of such instructions, and then the twist of a weary grimace move ever so slightly across his mouth.

"God knows I'm only pretending to be a Christian because I'm afraid I'm going to go to hell. How is that a healthy relationship with the Lord?"

"I know we've been strict with you ... We can't help wanting to protect you ...", Dad broke in, his voice serious and careful.

"But that isn't good enough, is it? That's not helping someone have faith ... It's substituting faith with rules and fear and then saying we can't even ask questions about any of it because we're women and we should be silent and just listen to the men."

"Darling ..."

"You and Mum are always going on about being good and not swearing, but actually there are situations – like my conversation this afternoon – when a swear word is exactly the right word of response. And you have *never* given me a good reason why I shouldn't have sex before marriage ...'

"Well ..."

"And saying that it says so in the Bible does not count. If it says it then there must be a good reason why ..."

I could tell that finally Dad was ready to meet me at last.

"Because it weakens marriage."

"Well ...", I sighed, my exasperated hands and shoulders sagging in deflation. "I have no response to that ... I can't know whether that's true."

"That's why you have to trust ..."

"Well, is it your experience?"

"I'm not claiming to be perfect, but I truly believe it's best to protect your marriage from the baggage you might take into it."

"You really think I've got no baggage, Dad? I've got *so* much baggage. All this religion is baggage. Nobody can be baggage-free ... Certainly no one with the upbringing we've had. It's not about sex – it's about the fear and naivety that Christianity has been cultivating ... for years. I loathe this God, I'm tired of Him ... He causes nothing but fear ... and slavery to rules ... I don't want to believe in it any longer."

I was shaking and crying with the relief of speaking truthfully at last, with the sense that somehow Dad was standing in for God: willing to have thrown back at him the words of love and freedom that had become so encrusted and mangled within me.

"Come here, Joanna ..." Dad gently pulled me down from the kitchen counter I was sitting on and enfolded me in his arms.

"I'm sorry, I'm sorry that I've been so strict with you over the years ... I've tried so hard to get it right and I can't help feeling I'm much to blame for your exhaustion and fear ... and I'm sorry."

I could hear the tears in Dad's voice, and as I sobbed into his chest, my words formed the most truthful prayer of conversion I'd ever prayed.

"I want to know if there is a God ... and if there is then She knows that I want to find Her and She's going to trust that I'm looking for Her even if I have to tear down a whole load of my religious pretence in order to get to Her ..."

Dad didn't react to the *she's* and *hers* and for a while the silence was broken only by stifled sobs.

"Joanna, will you forgive me for my part in this?"

"Yes ... but it isn't all you, not all of it."

"Listen, you go right ahead and apply to theological college. And don't worry about the money ... it will come together, but you're right you need to do this."

I might have left church right then, but that seemed churlish and it would also jeopardize my place on the youth work team, and so I carried on going, enjoying the friendships it held without worrying about my place in the holiness stakes any longer. When at the evening meetings the band led the congregated young people into some kind of ecstatic Jump-to-the-Lord-athon I sat at the side, my knees pulled up to my chin, watching the veins in their necks bulging with effort, the sweat glistening in drops across foreheads, the spit showering from mouths as they yelled "*Praise you Jesus*" and jumped as high as they could. Laura and Geoff were sitting near me too; I turned to Laura and we looked at each other. On the other side of her Geoff was gazing on and then he too caught my eye, his hand rubbing his chin as he harrumphed a smile at the madness taking place in front of us. I smiled back at him, convinced I no longer believed in the God they were jumping for. "*Coffee?*" Laura mouthed, and I got up with a nod, following her around the arc of frenzied noise out to the kitchen.

21

Turned Tables

That month was December and if I needed a chance to step back from church then my return to hospital for the final operation at least bought me a little respite. This time it would be a three-hour operation to construct a chin; nothing like the bone-splicing, flip-top facial reconstruction and rewiring I'd undergone just a few months earlier. No self-administering morphine button, or ICU blur; this time I was unceremoniously returned to an empty ward with my chin merely encased in plaster.

After the first operation I'd bumped into a girl from school who had remarked lazily 'I can't really see the difference ...' despite an almost two-centimetre shortening of my face. I wanted to lamp her. So although I knew that the chin job was going to complete Mr Harrison's work I didn't particularly expect it to be the most transformational operation of them all. It was only when Jane Addis walked into the ward for a surprise visit that I realized Mr Harrison's work might finally be done.

"Oh *Wow!*" she gasped. "You look completely different." She walked slowly over to my bed, her eyes fixed on my jaw.

"Seriously, that's incredible! Who is this girl?"

She bubbled with exclamations as I patted around my plastered, swollen jaw feeling for the difference.

And it was different. It was surreal even, when, for example, in January the new shop assistant started at the jumper shop with me and I recognized her from the year below me, in Curie House, at school.

"It's weird because it's not a common name but there was another Jo Jepson at school too ..."

"No ... I don't think there was."

There definitely wasn't.

"There was, she was in the year above me in Curie."

"Amy, that was me!"

"No, there was another one ... she had long hair and rode a bike ... she played the violin ..."

"Yes! ... Amy, that was me!"

Then my encounter with Emma, a girl with whom I'd studied A levels, in a class of 12.

"I was at school with your sister Joanna."

"Actually that was me, Emma ... *I* was in your English class."

"No, it was your sister ... Joanna."

"Emma, I'm Joanna, it's me you mean." She walked away, a spooked, expression on her face.

When I bumped into Dave, a man who used to go to our church, a man who'd known me since I was born and who looked at me with the polite bewilderment of a mistaken stranger, I realized I needed to start carrying around a passport photograph of my former self. Even I no longer recognized myself in the fleeting reflections as I passed shop windows, and when group photos were produced I had to search for myself, unable to immediately identify the neat new face that was now mine. My eyes no longer seemed to hang somewhere above the dwindling shape of my lower face, incidental to the incompatibility going on beneath them. Now my features were proportional, redrawn with definition.

It is a strange kind of invisibility, suddenly finding yourself unknown and unrecognizable, because you still feel like you. You still look out and see the world the same way, and carry with you the same expectations of it and the way it will respond to you. I met people I had known before and I expected to be met with the same attitude I'd always encountered from them – only now there was just neutrality, blankness. The proverbial clean slate on which we might chalk a different kind of rapport. It was the kind of invisibility that allows you to find out what people will make of you – who you are underneath your face. I was fascinated by the liberation; suddenly I was walking around with a face that had no commentary to it. I had not learned, through years of interactions, what people reckoned about these looks; so I couldn't assess this face. The swelling was subsiding so slowly that I just looked incredibly childish, like a fourteen-year-old in a twenty-year-old's body. Whatever had changed on the outside, surgery hadn't altered the way anxiety and inhibitions knitted me together on the inside. In unfamiliar situations I was still acting like the nervous, tongue-tied teenager I'd been at school.

It was with shyness too that a couple of weeks later, when I saw Matthew and Michael and a group of other boys from school in the pub, I went over to say hello. They had been in my tutor group and we had hung out sometimes when Louise was going out with Matt. I liked them – above all because neither of them had ever uttered a mean word to me. And so amidst their reactions of surprise and wonder at my newly re-made face I didn't see Nev standing behind them: a ghost of bullies past. For ghostly is how he appeared when laughing Matt turned to him and asked, "You've not seen Joanna since school?" He hadn't; but the memories of his belittling attacks from the row behind me in history lessons had stayed with me long after we had left. Now, as we faced each other again,

I couldn't remember any of the things he'd ever said to me, only a single memory: my hot tears, an awkward dash for the loos and Mr Thacker's surprise at my sudden, red-faced exit from his lesson.

Now it is Nev's face that burns, and me that watches the reaction. Matthew and Mike are laughing at Nev's silence; jeering the jeerer, enjoying his shame. Because it must have been a kind of shame: his head hangs down, then moves sideways in search of a way out. But there isn't one and he's stuck there having to take it. Matt looks at me expectantly. This is where I am meant to step into something other than shyness and embrace the power that Nev's embarrassment affords. This is where I get to gloat gratuitously because his slurs can no longer stick. But all I see is myself. Red-faced, silent, hoping that nobody else will see my humiliation, looking for an escape.

I should be enjoying this moment because the tables have turned, but now it's just like looking back at myself, seeing him feel the way I did. I say 'Hello Nev', then turn back to Matthew and Mike and suggest we head to the bar.

22

Captain Sensible

Friends at church hadn't known me before surgery; they were slightly puzzled by my need for a chin-job, and they were clearly uneasy at all its Hollywood associations being brought into their circles. It was difficult to know how enthusiastically plastic surgery should be appraised when there was no biblical guidance about it. But I was assured of their prayers all the same and when I returned to church after the plaster was removed the response to my transformation was mild; and I was spared the discomfort of feeling unduly vain. On an early January afternoon walk Rich made no specific comment except to show concern that I had recovered OK, and then that he preferred longer hair on girls in reference to my latest jaw-defining haircut – "It's more feminine." My disappointment was unalleviated by the knowledge that he had no idea of the significance this freshly bobbed hairstyle held. Perhaps he sensed that was the wrong thing to say after all as he changed the subject.

"How's it going with Geoff on Friday evenings then?"

I blushed at his interest.

"It's great, I really love it. And Geoff's a brilliant person to partner with. The guys we meet really respond well to him."

"Yeah, he's very much a father-figure, isn't he?"

"Yes, I wish some of those kids had fathers like him."

"You get on well with Joe too, don't you?"

It sounded more like an observation than a question.

"I have a lot of time for him. His situation is so sad, he's only a teenager … and he's homeless."

"Be careful there. He fancies you, Joanna."

I looked at Rich in surprise, then back to the mounds of grass over which we were picking our way. No … no! This was all wrong. It was Rich whose eye I was hoping to catch and now here he was dispassionately telling me I was attractive to the wrong person.

"I don't think that's an issue …" I tried falteringly. Heat crept across my cheeks.

In truth it wasn't something I'd ever had an issue with. Yet here it was like a misdirected parcel, wrongly addressed, being left at my door.

"Just be aware, OK? We're here to show them God's love."

"Yeah, definitely."

"Your passion and heart for the Gospel are so clear, Joanna, I think it's fantastic the rapport you've got with Joe and Leon. But those are the things that the Devil will use to twist and scupper the work we're doing."

The compliments crashed, and my romantic hopes with them. I felt like I was being outed as the handmaid of Satan.

But Rich seemed to be in no hurry to wrap up our chat and move on.

"So we are thinking of going to the cinema tomorrow evening. Can you come?"

It wasn't a date, but it was definitely progress; a chance to spend time with him without a whole lot of praying getting in the way. Only I felt further away from him than ever, as if I'd slipped down in his estimation. And so began the whir of my mind plotting ways to prove my worth to him: *be seen less with Joe and more behind the kitchen hatch making teas and coffees for everyone; be seen without make-up; start growing my hair; be heard praying better prayers in team meetings.*

I watched my mind playing out these scenarios.

Enough – whatever my beliefs now were they began with refusing to collapse myself into these cramped places of acceptability. Not for God and not for Rich.

I wouldn't avoid Joe and I would wear make-up to the cinema.

After the film, in which Rich sat next to me, we went back to the house he shared with two other guys, and ate pizza. It was the regular hangout in which rounds of coffee were brewed and half drunk, while Phil, Rich's younger housemate, coaxed the lads to complete stunt courses built out of furniture balanced against the open stairs and the girls offered motherly cautions while waiting for the boys to turn their attention towards them. Grace had started dating Phil and I watched her, coffee in hand, looking on at the antics, patiently waiting for some quiet time with him. I knew she was unlikely to get that time that evening. When romance did unfold – cautiously and prayerfully – it stayed safely within the bounds of the group. Breaking away into a private, exclusive coupledom would be dangerous, leaving lusts to fester unchecked by accountability to our brothers and sisters in Christ. There would be no staying behind when the rest of us made our move to leave.

"How's it going, Grace?" I smiled at her as she turned her eyes from Phil and met mine.

"Yeah, it's good thanks. I've moved halls and it feels way better this term."

"That's brilliant."

"How about you?

Mmmmm ... How about me? I had applied to theological college, wasn't sure I believed in God, and was pretty sure I didn't believe in church.

"Oh, I'm fine."

"How are things with Rich?"

"With Rich?" I exclaimed in a low whisper.

She widened her eyes and scrunched her mouth into a knowing smile.

"Umm, I'm not with Rich."

"Yes, but something's going on, isn't it?"

I sighed. I was so out of answers when it came to this kind of thing.

"Well, I have no idea."

"But you like him, right?"

"Yessss ... I like him."

"And he likes you."

"Really?" Now I might begin to get some answers.

"Yes, the boys have been teasing him about it, asking him when he's going to say something."

"Golly. Really?"

"Yes. Phil says he's just taking some time to pray about it and get some guidance."

"But I've not ... how ... why doesn't he just find out by talking to me a bit more?"

Grace laughed through her teeth. "Well he wants to know that it's the right thing before he gets involved."

"Ohhhhh ... so he wants some guarantee from God before he makes an investment ..."

She laughed again but I sat unsmiling, unsettled by this reminder of our efforts to avoid being too affected, tempted or tainted by life, and how we called it holiness.

Later, while hunting for remnants of pizza in the kitchen, Rich came and found me. I leaned against the counter and asked how he was. He smiled at me, holding my gaze, and we both knew that he had clocked my semi-clandestine chat with Grace earlier. There was to be no small talk.

"I'm doing a lot of praying, Joanna."

"That sounds significant."

"I want to know the Lord's heart … I sometimes I wonder if I'm falling in love with you and other times I'm not sure."

I was silent, caught up in the stomach-fluttering tantalization that love might come my way, and then the swift dropping dread that it might not come to pass after all.

I waited for him to ask me how I felt. This would be the moment, wouldn't it, to find out if his feelings were reciprocated, or whether I had been praying about it too? But there was no question; no space given for me to meet him with my answer. Instead he carried on.

"I don't want us to get involved if it's not going somewhere serious."

"Yes …" I had to look wise so I nodded sagely as if that made perfect sense to me. Then I blurted out.

"So how will we know?"

He smiled and drummed the palms of his hands on the counter as I continued.

"I mean if you don't know how you feel then how are you going to find out?"

"I know, it's hard." His voice suddenly took a convicted tone. "I just need time to pray about it, and hear God's answer. I want to be *Captain Sensible* here."

It might have been a word from the Lord or simply the church rumour-mill, but news of unfolding romances seemed to reach Justin somehow because the next Sunday evening he delivered a sermon on trusting in God and not leaning on your own under-standing. I'd heard it all before; that is until he illustrated it by referring to his girlfriend.

"I didn't know he was in a relationship …", I whispered to Laura incredulously.

She mouthed, "*Ruth*!"

I mouthed back, "*Wow*!" I had assumed he was the celibate type.

Justin carried on, "And in this relationship I'm in now, I hardly even kiss," which was remarkable as he was sounding undeniably passionate right now, "because while the world says you need to get to know your girlfriend physically in order to know if she's the one, I know that when God is in control of your life you don't need to worry about whether you will be compatible physically. And on my wedding night I know that we will be united in God's will for us physically and it will be *good*!"

Nobody laughed; this was no light-hearted end to his sermon. I peered over at Ruth to see how she was reacting to the broadcast of these intimate details, but she sat cross-legged on the floor looking up at Justin with unflinching trust. Justin's intensity was mesmerizing and as the band began to stir it was clear that people felt compelled to resubmit their relationships to God's sovereignty and control afresh. People were getting to their feet, singing with eyes shut and palms open. Phil and several other youngsters went forward to receive prayer. And a few feet away knelt Grace; her eyes closed, she was silent and still – probably handing her dreams of marriage back into God's hands.

A few days later Phil broke up with her, and I came to my senses. Rich and God might be drawing up their shortlist of candidates for the wife vacancy, but I was withdrawing my application. Captain Sensible was not the man for me.

23

Hippy Chick and Punk Boy

I didn't avoid Joe over the next few weeks and months, and I stopped trying to get to every prayer meeting I could to spend time impressing Rich. By the time my birthday came round the intensity of potential romance had ebbed away without word and I was spared from hearing Rich utter the words "I don't think it's right, I don't think it's God's will", and he was spared from hearing me say it wasn't my will either. We fell back into the ordinariness of the group and with it came quiet relief at having avoided a marriage where my vocation might only have been recognized in bearing children.

I wanted my birthday celebrations to be open to everyone, and I knew ice-cream would be a big draw for Joe. So word went round that the Häagen Dazs parlour would play host to my party. On the morning of my birthday I got talking to Dani, a hippy on the High Street, who offered to channel some specially charged energy through her crystals for me: I'd seen her before, and I knew she was homeless, but I couldn't pretend to want any of her energy-channelling wares and so I offered to take her for lunch instead. There we sat, rather improbably, eating quiches in the Regency

Fayre café, meeting the intrigued stares of respectable Cheltonians with smiles as we chatted about the underground rave scene being so much friendlier than nightclubs. She gave me a trinket for my birthday and I spontaneously invited her to my birthday gathering that evening.

It was only after my moment of spontaneity that I thought about how this would work out with Joe. Being a punk, Joe nurtured very particular affectations: a love of Sid Vicious, a fondness for piercings and tartan trousers and an unswerving disdain for hippies all contributed to his pursuit of authentic punkiness. Joe's ideology was about to be put to the test.

There were quite a few friends from church there already with Dani when Joe turned up. I hoped he wasn't off his face. And I hoped the presence of Leon and James alongside him wouldn't be an audience for him to play up to. Joe didn't notice Dani however: his diet of speed left him craving ice-cream and the venue was perfect.

"Oh yeah", he said, one hand in his pocket and the other one handing me a bundle of folded newspaper.

"Thank you Joe …", I smiled at the craziness of this presentation.

"Yeah, well I knew you liked her …" He looked away to the menu of ice-cream trying not to smile too generously.

Pulling back the excess of newspaper sheets I saw Alanis Morissette's "*Jagged Little Pill*" CD.

"You know it's nicked, don't you …?" Leon muttered, laughing quietly with James.

I had really, really wanted that CD, but when I picked up the card underneath I saw what the true gift was. Its carefully drawn scene copied from a Green Day album cover was neatly and painstakingly coloured in. And who knew where he'd got the crayons? When I opened the card some ripped sheets of an exercise book fell out. They were covered with Joe's neat writing; verses and songs, vocabulary and poetry beyond anything I'd imagined Joe would have come up with. I didn't ask if he'd nicked these words too. I assumed they were from Green Day or Sid Vicious. It didn't matter: they were Joe's gift to me. I felt a pinch of guilt that I'd invited Dani to join us – too late.

"Oh God, what's that hippy doing here?"

"I met her earlier today … she's really lovely, so I invited her too …"

"God I hate crusties."

"Well, you don't have to talk to her … Let's get some ice-cream – and thank you so much for my present and the card. I love them."

Joe slowly pulled his disdainful glare away from her and followed me to the ice-cream counter.

Later on I looked over to the table where Dani was: Joe was sitting next to her chatting away in his quiet, self-contained way. It was his second gift to me that evening.

* * *

There was one last party, at the end of the summer, before I went away to theological college. Mum and Dad vacated the house for the evening and now the music wafted throughout the rooms downstairs and out into the garden. Joe and I were sitting in the dining room on the floor. His tartan-clad legs stretched out in front of him and his back was flat against the wall. This was the person I dreaded leaving. Other friends – people with cars and independence – would come and stay in Bristol; we'd make weekends of it and our friendships would move with this change in seasons. But Joe had no fixed address and I had no car; emails and mobile phones had yet to emerge and rewire our social life. I had made Geoff promise that he would look out for Joe, and James and Leon, when I'd gone, but all the same I felt dreadful, unable to help them see how they were a large part of the reason I wanted to do this course and yet how guilty I felt for leaving.

Perhaps realizing that this would be our last conversation for a long while, Joe dropped his spiky facade, giving way to a confessional of fears, aspirations and unwelcome truths that he'd been bearing alone for too long. I wasn't a priest but perhaps right then I wished I had been; I wanted to let words of blessing cover him, I wanted to say "Go in peace because you are loved, important and known."

Three days later I left Cheltenham with the conviction that I was going to fit in far better among theologians than I ever had on a nursing course. But first impressions suggested otherwise when a member of staff approached Dad to offer him a warm welcome to the college. Certainly my father, with his sandals and his Marks and Spencer jumper, appeared the more probable candidate for a theological education, I thought, as I glanced down at the crisp white shirt, pencil skirt and kitten heels I'd chosen to wear. I'd never found much interest in fashion among church folk: modesty and presentability were the sartorial compass by which Christian women dressed, and wives seemed to dress their husbands, such was the apparent lack of interest in clothes displayed by men. But sitting there in the large, sunlit dining hall that first week of term I couldn't help but remark on the number of beards. "So it's true vicars really do have to have beards as well as sandals then?" I questioned the woman opposite me. She twinkled knowingly and explained that it was a sponsored beard-growing fundraiser for a leprosy charity out in Mozambique. I wondered whether growing the hair on my legs would be a welcome way for women to contribute, but decided against it and made a small donation to the beardy guys in my pastoral group instead.

Facial hair wasn't the only way in which appearances left me feeling strange. For the first week in morning chapel the doctrine and worship tutor, dressed in black cassock and white angelic surplice, walked us through the service of Morning Prayer, teaching us how to say it. At Emmanuel Church the vicar had only ever worn robes once every five years, when the Bishop was visiting. Yet here we were now, firmly in Church of England territory, with a dressing-up box of robes, being taught how to start and end sentences in unison, how to speak at the right pace and leave the correct length of silence between responses. I had never had to be taught; surely it was the Holy Spirit who led us in prayer and worship? I peeked through the rows at this priest-tutor, looking for signs of a personal relationship with Jesus. But there would be no eruption of spontaneous prayer or exhortations by which I might gauge his spiritual authenticity. I returned to my prayer book, trying to locate the canticle being recited, and realized I was lost.

I was 20 years old, in a college of mostly 38-year-old men training to be vicars. They had all done their thinking and reflecting, having been put through their paces in a searching process to discern their priestly vocation. They knew what their faith was about and why. They knew that they wanted to express faith and hope through a life spent ministering to the sick, the needy, the ordinary parishioners who lay two years down the line in a parish church somewhere. When they asked me why I had decided to study with them I had no clearly articulated answer, just a glimmering belief in God that lay buried somewhere beneath all the theology I'd inherited. When I was asked whether I wanted to be a vicar I didn't tell them that I was trying to overcome the inbred prejudices against women having roles beyond wife, administrator and Sunday school teacher. When, on my second day, one ordinand jokingly asked if I was injecting some glamour into the student community, I didn't say that I was experimenting with lipstick for the first time in my life, nor did I mention to anyone the surgery I had undergone and the anti-depressants I was still taking. I just took my place in lectures that began with a prayer; in a corridor of study bedrooms alongside matronly women of a certain age; and in a pastoral group of 12 students led by a twinkly-eyed professor of New Testament theology. On paper, it shouldn't have worked. And yet it did.

Living with the 44 other single students in Carter, the large house next to the college, I fell in love with these uncool men and women who ragged me like older siblings, and tickled my protestations by suggesting that I too might one day be ordained. They were intelligent, funny, dignified women and men whose faith was vibrant with authenticity despite the churchy robes they dressed in to lead prayer. Perhaps it was in their openness and humour that the robustness of their beliefs could be seen. The security of their faith showed up in the lightness with which they held the outward paraphernalia of religion. When the TV series *Ally McBeal* ended, the guys organized a fake requiem and black mourning bands were worn around college. Things that we would have called a prayer-meeting to deal with at church, here became fuel for satire.

And I found in my tutor wisdom and kindness and safety to ask the questions that had always been shushed away. In those first early weeks he called me in for my first pastoral tutorial, which was seminary-speak for "Come and tell me your story and why you're here."

For the first session I sat and sobbed and didn't say anything coherent. He invited me to sign up for another slot on the timetable outside his door, which I did, and resolved to pull myself together for round two. The second interview wasn't entirely tearless but his few, well-placed questions got enough information out of me for him to know what I needed.

"The thing is, Tim, it's as if I'm having an allergic reaction to this way of being Christian and I don't entirely know how to rid myself of it. I'm a product of all this so-called sound, correct teaching and doctrine. Yet when I look at the way I've lived my life it seems that it's all been an enormous attempt to appear to be good, to be on the Inside: one of Us rather than one of Them out there."

As I spoke I wanted to name the people I had tried over the years to drag over to my side of the fence: the Muslim boys, Louise and Jess, the lost and unsaved who existed out there on the wrong side of my judgements. And as I spoke it felt like I was taking bolt-cutters to the fence I'd built; I didn't want there to be a fence any more. Just like it was with Joe and me.

"The things that Jesus actually talked about to do with love seem to be about relinquishing those divisions, about letting go of the need to judge and deny and oppose. Those are the things I would want to be about if I was a Christian but I can't speak of them or share them because I'm not sure I've been changed by them myself. My measure of being a follower of Christ is whether I'm performing all the supernatural stuff ... healings and exorcisms and conversions ... and I don't do those things. I suspect I'm more like the hypocrites that Jesus warned about, the ones calling him 'Lord! Lord!' who never actually knew him.

(Pause for box of tissues to be handed to me.)

"I'd have walked away from all this religion months ago, but it's Joe and his friends – they have jolted me into not giving up. There's something about them, the crapness of their lives, their authenticity, their need for wholeness and purpose and hope and healing, their need to give of themselves and make a contribution to the world ... What matters to Joe isn't a particular brand of theology, it's knowing that God thinks he's OK even though he doubts he'll ever get his shit together.

"And there … there at that point, I run into the thing that I can't throw off: that God *is*. It's where I find I really do believe, because there all religiosity and formulas fail and demand a love that is so much more immense … it's like the shape of that need speaks of the presence itself … that's all I can call It … or Her … for now."

Tim was unhurried by the need to mop any of this up. He waited, smiled gently and then, in his soft, matter-of-fact voice, responded,

"Joanna, you know what you see going on with Joe is in part a reflection of your own story. You've been trying to respond to what those in authority have been telling you to be and to do your whole life. Now it's time to begin integrating, to listen to that still, small voice within and to begin trusting. What you're going to find is that these instincts aren't simply going to go away. The worry that you're not quite right, that you're not really meeting their expectations of holiness, goodness, attractiveness … these standards of perfection and righteousness aren't going to disappear. But you're in a new place here, it's a safe place to face these things … to begin choosing to trust that you have a lot to give, that you can be who you are and it's OK if that doesn't meet others' expectations. For now I think this season is about coming home to yourself."

I thought about that, about returning and staying with myself. He was right: this was an entirely safe place to do that. I was already beginning to get a sense of what it was like simply to inhabit my body as my strength grew after the operations. Cutting my hair, wearing clothes that I enjoyed wearing rather than voluminous things that just covered me and hid me.

I went back to my room and sat at my desk overlooking the woods: a beautiful, tranquil place to come home to myself as Tim had suggested. I wanted to do that, I wanted to be whole; face, heart and soul. I wanted to reclaim everything I had pledged, altered and manipulated to please others. I sat unmoving in the stillness. There within me was a desire to embrace who I was. All of it. The things I hoped I would be able to give; the memories that embarrassed and shamed me; the attempts to coerce friends into the arms of Jesus; the arms I'd raised and prayers I'd prayed to look holy; the good, potential wife material I'd tried to appear to be: sweet, subservient, not too pretty, not too threatening to a man's leadership. I recoiled but let myself feel every cringe of it. Every second I sat with it – with the revulsion, embarrassment, hopefulness, disappointment, allowing the memories and feelings to rise and be felt – was an act of faith, the opening of a door, enabling me to see that it all belonged, that something truthful could come out of these raw, misguided efforts. And as I stayed with every surfacing memory, I began to feel embraced by something beyond my own choosing. It was an awareness, resonating with unforced mercy, acceptance and love, covering me.

Next to the window through which I was staring hung a large pin-board, covered with photographs. I looked again at the arrangement, the highlights of life and friendships that I'd chosen to display.

Jane Addis and me on our third birthday.

Tim, Bear, Tamsin and Olivia hanging out the windows of our minibus somewhere on the road to Romania.

Seven-year-old Alastair with Rosalind in a headlock during a summer picnic.

Charlie Fox with the Malvern Hills rising up behind him.

Jane Addis hanging out of a tree at Smiley Week.

Dad hiking with mini-me on his back.

A portrait of Mum, tanned, gorgeous, happy, in Africa.

Only now could I see what was missing: I'd eradicated every picture with me as a teenager. No selfies to be seen, this presentation of my life had been arranged so that I was absent, the one behind the camera instead of messing around in front of it. A whole part of my life – of me – was missing.

There was a picture I needed to find, a photo that needed to be recovered and restored. I knew the exact one: Louise had taken it when we were fourteen and had posed together for black-and-white photographs. She looked perfect. Obviously I hadn't. I had hated that photo, and I knew that that was the picture I needed now. It took a while to sort through the disarrayed packets of snaps that I'd lugged with me to college in one large box, but eventually, with piles of photos fanned out in rows across my bed, I found the one I was looking for.

There she was: fourteen-year-old Joanna, sitting on a swing, hoping to be beautiful, just for one photograph, her wide, train-tracked smile tilted up to the camera. This is where healing begins. I took the snap and slipped it into a frame on my desk. This is how I begin to come home to myself and see what wholeness means. It means starting with her: with that frightened, hopeful girl, allowing love to cover her too. It means remembering her with compassion, because I'm the only person who can; the only person who can look at that photo and know the turmoil going on behind that toothy smile, and gather her up like a lost part of me. And so, with her looking up at me, I start to be restored, remembering her with all the kindness, understanding, affection and care I hadn't felt before. She's with me, I want to declare.

There was another photo, among the piles, that also caught my attention. It was a picture of me with Jane, Louise and her twin sister, Jess, when we were seventeen. I'd invited them over for a dinner party – my first attempt, I served home economics cottage pie with Lambrusco – and we had felt incredibly grown up. I was wearing the suede miniskirt so cursed by my failed attempt to get into TIME nightclub. Three years on, it was still hanging in my wardrobe. I looked at the picture, at my hope of being transformed from gawky seventeen into something lovely and womanly. It was time for the suede skirt to be worn, to be redeemed, to be danced in all night long.

At the top of Bristol's Park Street, between Sainsbury's and Lloyds Bank, was – and hopefully still is – an anonymous, brown, metal door leading down to the onomatopoeically named Lizard Lounge. A cheesy dive, loved and packed out by students almost every night of the week: it was perfect for my plan. Ground was going to be broken, dances reclaimed and trainee priests set free to find their inner J-Lo. I put up posters around the common room, canvassed the women on my corridor in search of a critical mass, and generally let it be known that the following Friday night we would be having a group outing to the Lizard Lounge.

Possibly because these 30, 40 and 50-something singles knew that there would be few occasions left for disco dancing oblivion once they held public office and had a dog collar around their necks, or because there really was safety in numbers, I was joined that evening by 22 vaguely glammed-up ordinands – at least one pair of legs was clad in leopard-skin print – for divine takeover of the Lizard Lounge. We formed a queue at the doors and I stood at the front of it, ready to oversee the admittance of my gang. No ID was demanded and this time the slightly fazed reaction of the bouncers was caused by my insistence that they had to let every single one of us in because we were all together and it wasn't often that theological colleges had outings to nightclubs. It worked: even the guys in anoraks – beige, not leopard-printed – were admitted. We were in and, being unfashionably early, we had the whole, though small, dance floor to ourselves.

Hours later, when I asked the DJ for a shout out to the Church of England clergy, he thought he hadn't heard right, but after repeatedly yelling in his ear that there really were a large number of trainee vicars on his dance floor he clearly felt this was a niche following which, as a DJ, he ought to nurture. Throughout the night there were special dedications to all the vicars in the house followed by thoughtfully chosen tunes he felt would be appropriate for us.

Like a Virgin

Faith

Love Shack

Like a Prayer

You Got the Love …

And we had. We loved it. It was my Eric Liddell moment. We danced until 3 a.m. and I felt God's pleasure.

In February came another outing. This time it was for our pastoral group to head across the nearby Welsh border, to a convent for a Retreat Day. No suede mini-skirts here, we turned up bundled in woollies and hats, taking seriously the warning that it would be cold. Up in the retreat house we were shown to a long, creaking, dark room with worn rugs, a piano at one end, and crocheted doilies on the dark, old coffee tables. Freshly picked grasses and foliage leaned out of small vases on the window sill and mantelpiece and sideboards. Outside the window stretched a long meadow that a doughty nun seemed to be taming from her perch atop a ride-on mower, her wimple blowing out behind her.

The nun who came to lead our day seemed less doughty, awkward even, maybe unaccustomed to looking 12 strangers in the eye and talking at them for a whole day. But looks can be deceiving. With a warm, slightly fading voice she invited us to hand over our watches for the next few hours and tune into a different rhythm. Wondering what that rhythm would be, I popped my pink baby-G watch into the hat, intrigued.

A bell tolled plaintively and we were led down through the

meadow and into the convent's chapel. Silence; winter sunlight resonating on rosy stone; the odd black-robed figure shuffling books into place; the polished curves of a Christ-figure hanging on the cross, lovingly carved out of wood, the focus of the room. More nuns; candles being lit; readings found; silver accoutrements placed; sisters taking their places; eyes closed.

Silence.

A bell tolled again, followed by a tinkling bell, and nuns, with varying degrees of effort, pulled themselves to their feet.

"The angel of the Lord brought greetings to Mary and she conceived by the Holy Spirit: Hail Mary full of grace, the Lord is with you, blessed are you among women and blessed is the fruit of your womb Jesus ..."

Uh oh. Praying to Mary: it was a big no-no for evangelicals to put any mediator besides Christ in the way of our communication with the Lord. It was up there with dabbling in wizardry. Only now I was more preoccupied by the sight of a young woman in the front row, just a little older than me perhaps. She had been ringing the bell with her back to me so I hadn't seen that she was young. Now she'd taken her place in the pew and I could see that she was still a novice; her habit was grey instead of black like the sisters', and she had no headdress. She was also the only person who could sing. Beside the fact that the musical bits of the liturgy might as well have had every note chosen at random, it was sung three octaves too high for all the croaking, deaf, elderly women whose job it was to sing them. It was terrible. Except for the novice's clear voice that gave the rest of us visitors the chance to see what the tune should have been.

The service continued with almost studied lack of intonation; no excitability, no attempt to try and rouse the congregation into some kind of manufactured psycho-spiritual thrill. It was almost as if each nun was saying the words and they all just happened to be in the same room at the same time. I was fascinated, with the kind of fascination you get when something is awful but being done with a straight face all the same and you're waiting for someone's face to crack. But nobody's did, until we realized that we should follow the sisters up to make an arc around the plain, stone altar to receive the wafer and the wine. And then a small, bespectacled sister, with a bleeping hearing-aid in need of new batteries and tufts of grey hair that looked as if it might have been cut with a knife and fork shooting out from under her slipping wimple, turned and broke into a strong, welcoming smile and gestured for me to come and stand beside her. That was all. Her opening arms, her unfussy welcome, her unconcerned return to silent devotion all simply allowed us to take our place in the service, free to get the words or gestures wrong, free not to be able to follow what was going on, to stay standing when the rest of them knelt, or to remain upstanding when everyone else bowed low before the cross. Their welcome was simple, wide and genuine and absolutely devoid of any effort to cajole, correct or impress us. They truly were, in a very ordinary, unotherworldly way, about Something Else.

It was something I didn't get, but by the end of the day I wanted to know more. Their lack of frothy spirituality, the realization that they had hung days, years, decades of their life on this simple, quiet unspectacular rhythm of worship, was fascinating and compelling. It spoke of something unseen but undoubtedly deep-rooted in truth, for there was little else to commend this spartan way of life and worship.

So at the end of the day, when we had finished whittling hand-held crosses on the verandah whilst listening to the quiet, warm observations with which Sister Mary Jean answered our questions, I asked her if I could come back and stay longer. "Well, we have people to come and live with us for three months at a time, as Alongsiders ...", her eyes creased with a smile stretching across her face and lifting her striking, high cheekbones, and her face shifted as if uneasy with one-to-one encounters. "You could write to Mother Gillian and tell her you'd like to explore this ... perhaps in your summer holidays?"

We drove away from the convent down windy, forest-lined roads, Sue and Guy already laughing, singing, "How do we solve a problem like Joanna?" at the prospect of my summer spent in a nunnery. Over the next few months letters arranging my visit went back and forth between Mother Gillian and myself. My twenty-first birthday came and went, and there were only three weeks left of term and a long summer stretching out silently ahead of me. I couldn't wait.

Then, that evening, came a phone call from Laura in Cheltenham. It was Joe. He was dead. He'd choked on his vomit; his body was found six days later.

24

The Time of Your Life

I couldn't go anywere. It was the end of term: valedictory services were being prepared; choir rehearsals were squeezed between services, farewell tea parties and dinners; rooms needed to be cleared and outstanding essays finished. The college was buzzing with celebration and excited families preparing to move to their new parishes. And I watched it all through a blur of free-falling tears. I was sickened: by the thought that Joe was dead, by the thought that I'd not seen him since I'd left, by the thought that he was alone like that when he died. Unseen and unfound. I sat through choir rehearsals letting the music wash over me, unable to open my mouth and sing one note. The words of hymns and prayers sounding around me as the leavers' futures were gathered up and dedicated and blessed provoked fresh floods of tears as I saw again the loss of Joe's future. In the end I stopped trying to hide and wipe them away and nobody else tried to either. Even in the flow of a community leaning with anticipation into new futures, students stood still with me and waited with me for the reverberations of grief and loss to be absorbed afresh all over again.

Someone posted a card under my door,

"Joanna, I think that God is bigger, much bigger than our human efforts, than our inadequacies. He has to be. So we don't have the answers, but God is just and loves the weak."

I was devoid of answers. Joe dying was not the way it was meant to go. That wasn't the story I wanted to be part of. It wasn't the hope I had hoped for him. So how could it have been allowed to happen? If I loved Joe this much then how much more did God love him? But I didn't have the energy to pound God with my "whys?"; instead I let them wash down my face in tears of disbelief.

Joe's funeral was a couple of days after term ended. Rosalind, who had met him several times, offered to come with me and so together we drove out to the town where he had lived. The church was full, the vicar, white-haired and robed, appeared utterly swamped by the rabble of young people, all looking as if they were caught somewhere between grief and shock. We slipped into a row next to Geoff and another couple from the youth work team, and watched as the coffin was carried in.

It wasn't just the sight of his coffin that shook me. It was Leon, anorak falling off one shoulder, struggling to take the weight of the coffin as he buckled in his own stunned sorrow. His eyes were bloodshot and he looked worse than I had ever seen him. He looked as if he was about to go the same way.

I don't remember much about the service; just the haunting words of Joe's parents, "If only we could turn back the clock." And then the clear melodic chords of Green Day's song, "Good Riddance (Time of Your Life)", broke into the silence of the hushed congregation, the words following him as he was carried out to the graveyard.

Outside, next to his grave, I was joined by Leon and James. Leon stood by me mute, watching open-mouthed and red-eyed as the electric guitar of blue flowers disappeared under the shovel-loads of dry soil. And James stepped up in his smart suit and ushered forward his shy girlfriend to be introduced. He told me about the college course he was on, the A-levels he was working towards, having messed them up back at school, and his ambition to become a vet. And then he said, "I hope you become a vicar – so you can marry me and Amy."

I stared at him. I didn't even know the word vicar was in his vocabulary. I looked at him and then at his girlfriend, trying to compute where this idea had just come from. How could he know this?

I had shrugged and laughed off so many comments from friends at college about being called to ordination. It was easy: I told them I wouldn't be jumping on their bandwagon. It didn't mean anything that trainee vicars suggested I think about training to be a vicar; being a vicar was what was on their mind.

But this was James talking – James who didn't have anything to do with Anglican clergy. I'd always wanted to come back to these lads. Now I was here – not in the way I'd expected or wanted – but I had come back and I couldn't shrug off James's words.

25

Tractors and Silence

There's a kind of romance that obscures the reality of convent life. Something about the nuns' silence and their identically crisp, stark, black-and-white habits that makes it really hard not to imagine all the lovelorn desires and tragic secrets and naughty rebellion that are probably being harboured underneath. That is how I saw it anyway. Based on a childhood overdosing on *The Sound of Music* and occasional visits to a nearby manor house inhabited by labradors and nuns who glided like shadows from afternoon tea to their wrought-iron-gated chapel, I was ill-prepared for the reality that lay ahead of me at Ty Mawr.

At first it all seemed to be as I anticipated. An ancient sister was on the front lawn tending the roses when Mum and I arrived. She creaked slowly over to us with a trug under one arm and rasped, 'Hello, you must be Joanna.' Then turned and led us off to the room where I was going to live for the first month of my stay. It was a charming room, above the front porch, overlooking the roses and front lawns and the fields rolling away from the end of the path beyond. I unpacked my suitcase and saw a card left for me:

A very BIG welcome Joanna. Just be and sleep and know. Love, Mary Jean

On the desk lay a sheet of paper. It was a timetable of all the offices of prayer.

7 a.m.	Morning Prayer
8.45 a.m.	Terce
12 p.m.	Mass
5.30 p.m.	Vespers
8 p.m.	Silent prayer
8.30 p.m.	Compline

At least they weren't in the habit of getting up for chapel at 3 a.m.

And so the rhythm of this quiet new life went, day after day after day after day. In between chapel I was assigned to work on the land surrounding the convent, with Martin, the gardener. Mornings were spent cleaning the guesthouse under Sister Veronica Ann's supervision. This was incredibly fortuitous, first because she was the only other extrovert there, and second, being a good distance away from the convent, we were free to indulge in very chatty coffee breaks on the verandah. I told her stories about Joe, and about nights spent dancing at the Lizard Lounge to which she would rumble ho-ho-ho's of laughter and exclaim, 'I mean to say, how gorgeous! How simply gorgeous!'

And she told me about her journey from South Africa to Wales, and about her 50 years at the convent, and the days when sisters weren't allowed to go into other establishments, not even fish and chip shops, and how she once had to stand outside a chippy eating her newspapered meal in a downpour. Sister Veronica Ann was a force of nature; the kind of tough nut that would dig through snow drifts to clear the road to the convent in harsh winters and think nothing of mowing a full field of hay between changing the sheets in the guest house and attending to bed-bound sisters in the convent. She was awesome; I wanted to be her when I grew up.

So when Martin, told me I was going to learn to drive the tractor it looked like my dream might come true. In a cloister hung photos of the sisters stretching back to the first early days in the 1920s and the founding sister, Mother Gwenvrede, could clearly be seen atop the very same grey Ferguson tractor I was about to helm. There was a strange pride in taking my place high up on the little seat that had been sat on by generations of indomitable women. They clearly didn't dally with an ideal of womanhood that involved validation by husbands or children. Marriage and motherhood might well be a sacrifice but it seemed nothing compared to the breath-taking pursuit of truth to which nuns gave themselves. Climbing up onto the little black seat was like joining a long line of women who had fearlessly battled earth and soul and I pondered whether one had to be a nun in order to follow in their footsteps.

"The thing is," I confessed to Martin as we raked up the hay I'd mown, "I just don't think I could stop talking for long enough to be a nun. Last night, when Sister Susan walked into the kitchen during the Great Silence, she glared at me and said 'You're looking very guilty Joanna' – even though I'd managed to stop discussing hot chocolate with Judith *before* she came in! Somehow these nuns just *know* stuff."

"Are you thinking about the novitiate then, Joanna?"

I definitely wasn't. I had been very sure for the months leading up to my visit never to say "I'm never going to be a nun." There were too many stories told by ordinands who had once said I'm never going to be a vicar and then ended up with a vocation. I had been more careful than that. The problem was that I had declared far and wide that I was never going to be a vicar. And it had been an easy suggestion to shake off until James suggested it.

"When James said to me, 'I hope you become a vicar', it was like a call I couldn't refuse."

"Well, it sounds like you've got to listen to that, then, doesn't it" he said, stirring his mug of tea.

"Yeah, it all seems so planned, as if God has sneaked ahead of me and put everything in place ... my stay here, the space to grieve for Joe, the space to listen ... at least the space to learn to stop talking ..."

Martin didn't say anything; he just had a wry smile on his face as he leaned on his rake, sipping his tea, watching as if waiting for me to get the message.

"Working with Joe and Leon and James made me so restless to go to theological college, I thought I would learn things there that would bring me full circle back to them, that I would be able to work with them more usefully than being a Friday and Saturday evening do-gooder."

"As long as it was anything but being a vicar."

"Yep. And now James has told me that's exactly what he needs me to be. I ... I just cannot ignore it." I grimaced.

"And? What's so bad about it?"

"I don't know ... well, I guess it's just so dowdy and frumpy. I mean, even when James said what he said, the second thing that went through my head – after the stream of pulsing exclamation marks – was 'I can't! I don't look like a vicar! I don't have a beard, grey hair or a fairisle jumper.'"

"And what have looks got to do with it?"

OK, so when it was put like that the answer had to be nothing. It was one of the tenets of faith I now lived by, that looks would no longer bar me from places, people or dance floors. That is, until vicars were mentioned. Then I collided headlong with all the lingering distortions and prejudice that still lurked, unexorcised, in my mind. I would have fought like a wild thing had one fluorescent spike of Joe's hair been combed down by a po-faced preacher man or if an assailant had dared to spit again at Alastair's face. But when it came to me the self-image in my head was still held hostage somewhere between 1 Peter 3.3 and the vital statistics of an original 1990s supermodel. Becoming an androgynous vicar would mean the demise of *all* femininity – and what that really meant was being a spinster. Single; unchosen; game over. In fact the only way I could see to make that situation OK would be by becoming a nun. If I end up a spinster vicar maybe I could become a nun when I'm 30 as a kind of back-up? Maybe. Maybe I'll have stopped talking too much by then?

I decided Martin wasn't the kind of guy I could have this girl chat with. In fact, as I looked around chapel during Evening Prayer, I wasn't sure there were many people there with whom I could discuss this conflict. But I was wrong. A few days later Novice Joy revealed she had jumper envy. My bright pink, green and blue striped Boden knit had caused a sister to stumble.

"I love your jumper … it's so joyful, I love seeing you wearing it in chapel against our sea of black and white."

"Really?! Well, you can have it …" Then, realizing the uselessness of this offer, "I mean, you could have it and wear it on your day off."

"Oh no, nooo … I like seeing it on you, it's so you! I just wish we could have brighter habits. Why can't we have multi-coloured habits? What's so holy about black?!"

She was laughing, but I was relieved to get even a hint of sartorial awareness from a nun.

"Well, I'll design you a habit that's made in a colour to suit you. I'd love to do that. You find me the pattern, I'll make a joyful collection of red, green and purple habits and before you know it chapel will be a brighter place …We'll be like silent Gay Pride."

"Oh my goodness … That would be fantastically subversive."

"Do you think it would feel more feminine if you wore colour?"

"Ooooh, I don't know … maybe a bit … I think it's all the glumness that I shy away from and the association of piety with gloom. The skies are grey enough here in winter. But then I don't suppose you become a nun to wear particularly pretty clothes …", she mused, still smiling.

"It's so funny to hear you express concern about the lack of colour in your clothes."

She replied with an ambiguous "Mmmmmm".

"I mean you guys are nuns and your expression of femininity is so awesome … it seems to go way beyond what you wear."

"Well I suppose it does. But I'm still aware of myself as a clothed person", she said wistfully.

By now we'd taken off our trainers and sandals and were stretching our toes into the cold pond at the bottom of the field.

"Joy, I've got such a hang up with clothes and vocation … I've heard a blaring call to the priesthood, like a force of truth I can't swerve away from … but …"

"But bad clothes?!"

"Awful. Becoming a woman vicar …", I groaned, and wondered how many years it would take for us to drop the gender prefix and the implication that it was a man's job.

"Dreadful!" she mocked, chuckling, her eyes scrunched shut against the sun.

"Surely the fact that my biggest stumbling block is vanity makes me entirely unsuitable for ordained ministry."

She laughed again, looking at me expectantly.

"I suspect that that and all your other reasons are the very things that will make your ministry worthwhile …"

She was sprawled out, feet dripping with water, flattening the overgrown grasses with her outstretched frame.

"What's it going to take, Joanna?" Her voice was so lilting and gentle. "You've been looking for a way to return to those guys in a useful way. Now they've told you themselves that they want you to be their priest."

"But I don't like the answer: it clashes with the picture of life that I've pieced together in the scrapbook of my mind."

"Something's going to have to give … and I just wonder what it is going to take for you to give it …"

So far it had taken James's simple request. And now it was my need to be in control that remained, and the decision to trust that God wasn't waiting for me to grow a beard and become a man. The decision to believe – in order that one day I might come to see what God had been creating all along. Choosing to let go of all the things in my head that I thought I ought to be in order to please false gods, parents, peers, preacher men and potential husbands …

It would take the giving up of all these things.

I didn't know how, but in the quiet, unshakeable dignity of these women I felt I had seen strength of purpose and authenticity and womanliness that went beyond all I knew about feminism. There was no sense that they were reacting to anything or trying to disprove the fearful possibility that men were indeed the preferred half of the population. Nor was there ever any squirm of innate, apologetic behaviour so rife among the circles of girls I'd known. Just their ease in inhabiting the space that was theirs, as if their spirits expanded into the full possibility of any given moment. I found myself constantly and unexpectedly struck by the beauty of these women. They were elderly, with skin that sagged away from cheek and jaw bones, and facial whiskers that hinted at their years, and yet that isn't what I saw when I looked at them. It was the liveliness: a radiance in their eyes that made you feel you had been drawn into a dance with them, and made you want to join in and see where it would take you.

I wanted to sit with Sister Cara soaking up the intelligence of this woman who had worked to help break the Enigma Code. I was intrigued by all that had led Sister Gillian here. I could have stood doing the washing up all evening just to spend time listening to beautiful Sister Clare, or to watch what Sister Mary Janet would do or say next. When the global beauty brands declared that "Beauty comes from within", these nuns were what they were talking about. And yet here they were, living lives that gave no opportunity to test their sense of self against the approval of men. Their strength was in surrender, not to patriarchs or illusions of ego, but to something else. I couldn't yet tell what or how, but it was obviously a gazillion worlds away from cover girls and cultural myths about woman's worth resting in the hand of the man that chooses her.

Soon after my arrival a new Reverend Mother had taken office, and this time it was to be the nun who had led our retreat day in February. The newly elected Mother Mary Jean epitomized this magnetism. She was ageless, compelling and fragile. Her eyes seemed to shy away from you but her presence opened up a place of complete safety and compassion; complete enough to hold anything. I wanted to have time with her more than anyone, I wanted to hear how she had thrown off her doubts, and the *shoulds* and *oughts* of subservience to false gods. I wanted to know what illusions she had relinquished. But it wasn't clear how I would get an opportunity to talk to her. The only talking times of the week were Thursday supper, Saturday tea and Sunday lunchtime. I waited for a chance to bump into her, to explain the entangled muddles of my soul and ego and have her wisdom piece me back together.

The days went on, a rhythm of work, prayer and meals, and I waited for an opportunity. A mass was said for Joe and through the storm of tears I believed once again that – wherever It was and whatever It was like – Joe was held and loved and free.

* * *

Then life carried on and I got on with my chores. I painted the inside of a tiny chapel in the woods. I sat in silence and darkness before Compline each evening. I hoped for interesting visitors to arrive. I waited for something to happen, something to break the monotony. The waiting became boring, and then turned into a growing restlessness; like having itchy blood.

Within days it had manifested as the need to run. Anywhere. Anywhere where there was normality, chatter, fast food, shops, TV and inconsequential decisions to be made. My nun impersonations continued but behind closed eyes I was thinking up devious plots to get away. Offering to take the community car off to fill it up with petrol in a stealth bid to fill up my bag with magazines, snacks and cigars and a bottle of port. Hijacking interesting guests at the retreat house and demanding they share cheese and wine with me and tell me things about the world outside; or better still give me a lift Out Of Here.

I found my sights straining towards anything in the week that would be different, eventful, sociable. Things like driving Sister Jeanne to a dentist appointment where I could sit reading magazines in the waiting room became the highlight of my week. I counted the days until the next Thursday evening, when we would be able to talk at supper and round off the meal with chocolate and beer. I longed for Monday recreation evenings when we would go down to the print house and sit looking out at the view whilst listening to a classical CD chosen by Sister Gillian. I could feel all my expecta-tions and energy being pent up, ready to seize and consume both cake and conversation alike at tea on Saturday afternoons, just to assuage the loneliness and boredom for an hour. Then, hearing the 5.15 p.m. bell toll, I would realize it was over and whatever I was really waiting for and looking forward to hadn't happened and now there would just be silence again. And another chapel service.

Another chapel service in which I would sit and wonder what I was doing, and feel tears over Joe falling once again, suddenly and easily. His picture was propped up in my stall next to my prayer books. I looked down at him: gone. Everything felt empty and depressing. Joe's unfinished life; this searching, gnawing, boring, empty existence with nothing to look forward to; this silent, bare chapel with all its bad singing and holy ordinariness, watched over by the carved, dead figure of Jesus. There was nothing even slightly romantic about it. No wonder there were so few extrovert nuns. There was nothing here. The silence and stillness just reminded me of the emptiness, like a diet reminding you of your hunger.

I took the bike that Sister Clare had lent me and, after Compline, when the Great Silence had begun, I would creep out to cycle round the lanes exploring in the late light of the summer evening. But nothing silenced me. This silence that I was watching, pacing through daily, trying to surrender to … despite all its power, it couldn't silence the noise in my head. My mind swung between grief, longing and the demons that rose up in between. It was so confusing. I had come here because these women so powerfully reflected a God I actually believed in. A God who wasn't frothy, or in need of our jumping and shouting or pretence. A God who was big enough to hold everything; our shadow side, our incompleteness, our pretences. A God who welcomed everyone and everything we brought with us. Of course I thought I would find peace here … a convent is where people go for peace, right?

And yet, against the backdrop of all this silence I wasn't at peace: my brain was winding on an unstoppable roller-coaster of wretched thoughts. An endless loop of longed-for escapades or imagined dramas in which I would tell Cliff to repent of his misogynistic theology and go and get some proper theological training for himself; I would chide Janet for colluding with evangelical patriarchy and not being the role model we girls had needed her to be; I would line up every preacher man from my childhood and lambast them for the blasphemy with which they had used the Bible to subjugate women, patronize non-Christians and frighten Christian youngsters into submission with threats of hellfire and damnation. And, when my mind had exhausted those fantasies, it would lurch on to torment me with moustached images of myself, aged 30, cassocked and surpliced in tent-like robes, a wedding ring nowhere to be seen.

The worst thing about feeding on a mental diet of blame, resentment and fear is that you can begin to enjoy it. These things become companions. Like a dog with a juicy bone, my mind relished the seduction of these dramas. Alone, wishing I wasn't quite so addicted to this company of inner demons, I tried to concentrate on the words of the psalm in front of me; or the banister I was polishing; the bed I was making. Or the fruit I was picking. But I couldn't switch off the stream of thoughts and I returned to the scullery with bucketloads of rhubarb, and saw Sister Joan try to stifle her alarm at the sight of an entire patch of picked rhubarb laid out in mountains across the counter space, wondering where on earth to freeze it all.

Finally, weeks later, Mother Mary Jean knocked on my door. She came and sat on my bed and asked me how I was. I told her. She clasped her hands and looked off to the side as she talked, as if she was listening to something else and relaying it to me. Her warm rasping voice was accompanied by a compassionate smile every now and then.

"The silence can feel terrifying, I think. We feel our defences and hear the voice of our monkey mind scrabbling between worry and fear ... but that's the gift of silence too ... it creates space for us to listen and to be."

"But I'm so frustrated by what I'm seeing about myself. It's all I can do to stop myself escaping to the pub for an evening just to get some TV and mindless distraction from myself."

"Keep listening, keep listening ... the gift is all there. What you're coming up against are your false comforts; you have to see those so that you can be freed from them."

Her voice was so calm as if the grip of one's ego was something to be gently shrugged off, but then she continued:

"This pain is the only thing strong enough to shift the masks and defences we have around ourselves. Our ego is afraid to be without all these comforts, it's afraid of that kind of nakedness. It can feel like it's you failing, but these things are all in the mind. It's just the voice of your monkey mind, they're not actually you."

She watched me for a moment, waiting for the words to settle within me.

"God's brought you here to begin revealing what you are, to allow all the stuff that gets in the way back at home and college to fall away. It's uncomfortable, but let the silence hold you."

I didn't speak.

"Just stay present to it all, you don't need to overcome or stop these thoughts or the desire to escape ... just sit with it."

As she got up to leave I asked her how she'd known to come and see me.

"Oh, I heard a whisper."

"Who? Who told you?"

She fluttered her fingers up next to her ear. "Oh, nobody ... I just heard a little whisper."

The next day a cassette player and tapes of Mozart's piano concertos were left outside my room. Alongside them was a framed picture of Rembrandt's *Return of the Prodigal Son* and a note from Mary Jean: *I thought these might be good companions for you.*

In the company of a prodigal son, 13 nuns and a gardener, I promised God that I wouldn't bolt. I stopped trying to fill the emptiness, or trying to achieve anything out of it. Instead I felt it. I allowed myself to rest into it, letting myself be, no matter how clanky or hollow that felt.

When it all felt like a monumental waste of time, I thought "So let's waste time."

When I found myself mentally throttling preacher men, I let go.

When I got twitchy and felt hidden away without any measureable props of success, I thought "Yes" – and relished the apparent insignificance of it all.

When temptation to imagine a better version of myself overtook me, I looked down at the holes in my trainers and the soil under my nails. I felt my back pressed against the wooden stall, the thin cushion padding my backside and the sound of my quivery voice not quite managing to follow the tune of whichever hymn we were trying to sing. This was how I returned to myself and made myself at home in the present moment.

This was the only place I could truthfully encounter God or anyone else. Not in memories and reactions to past pain or in thoughts about the future, but right here in this place, among these women who got jumper-envy and had their own brand of unacceptable bits: like bad tempers and impatience. Like loud tutting at the sister who had wafted obliviously past a note of instruction that had been left for her by another sister. Or the huffs and puffs of annoyance when Sister Cara failed yet again to tune her hearing-aid in to the correct loop and subjected the rest of us to 30 minutes of high-pitched whistling. Or the look of fury that one sister gave another when she overlooked the large sign saying "Chalice Bearer" left in her stall for immediate attention. Novice Joy's mouth would ripple with a smile, her gaze directed safely away from mine, and I suspected there were chuckles in the heavens too.

The quiet wasn't spoilt by irritations and jealousies; the nuns' humanity made it strong enough for everything just to be held and loved. These women were willing to be honest about their humanity and they lived expecting God to dwell within them anyway. They weren't trying to create the magic of silence in order to appear holy; they were saying Yes to it. Day after day, year after year, their whole lives were a great *Yes* to the silence; to allowing all things to be heard and held in it; to being stripped bare by it; to discovering that underneath it all there is only love.

And so, when I stopped being so frightened by the silence, I saw that it was the only thing that would peel back enough layers to help me see the truth that underneath it all is love.

And I saw that the silence wasn't frightening: it was strong, it *was* Love. A vast Love revealing my nakedness and emptiness, my insignificance and poverty, so that I could be covered and clothed at last.

26

Stealth Nettle Farming

"Into your hands I commend my spirit
For you have redeemed me Lord God of truth."

"Into your hands I commend my spirit
Keep me as the apple of your eye."

"Hide me under the shadow of your wing
Into your hands I commend my spirit."

The words arched across the space in chapel each evening, gently sent out from one side before being responded to by the sisters on the other.

Into your hands I commend my spirit.

The words had started to sound rhythmically in my mind, becoming a prayer that I didn't so much think as just hear, rising up over and over again. When my mind swung from worry to fear to doubt like a boat bobbing up and down on the water I returned to those words, letting them anchor me.

Into your hands I commend my spirit.

It struck me that these were the last words Jesus prayed as he hung on the cross. I looked up from my stall at the carved figure of Christ, his head falling forward: dying. These weeks of silence, of facing my fears, efforts and grievances, were a kind of death, a letting go of all the important things I'd thought life was about. It made me face the anxious unwanted thoughts that goaded me to react to them, triggering me to busy myself with schemes to avoid the dreadful fate they suggested. What would I become if I didn't fight them off by proving that I was a success – whichever image of success I chose? It was like spiritual vertigo; a feeling of falling, without knowing if there was a harness or arms to catch me.

But when I looked up at Christ, up on the wall in the dimming light of the evening, I saw the ultimate in epic fails.

Into your hands I commend my spirit.

That Christ who died and rose again to save us – I was so familiar with the words and the bit about being saved that I'd skipped the bit about dying. That's what faith was for us: about believing that Christ had died and risen for us so we could get into heaven. But in all my efforts to Be Saved and Avoid Hell I'd missed the fact that something has to die before new life can blossom – something in me. Now here it was: the picture of Jesus surrendered, out of control, undefended, dying. It wasn't a piece of correct doctrine to be spouted; it was the way to follow, the surrender of all my agendas and control and self-images. I stared up at the cross with the figure on it, gathering me into its story. What I'd always taken for some Anglo-Catholic ornament was now finding me, drawing me in with its whispers of life and hope.

And I heard the whisper of my reply: *whatever that new life is, I'll say Yes to it.*

It was a moment of surrender: a significant moment but just another moment of surrender all the same. It was becoming clear to me that I didn't just do it once aged five in Glories and tick the box; it was to be a life-long journey. Letting go in order to be made a little more whole, again and again and again.

That particular evening I knew that it would mean returning to college with a view to begin discerning with my tutors and my Bishop whether I had a vocation to the priesthood. I knew that it would be a rigorous process, which might take a couple of years. But all this procedure and testing seemed like a matter of course, because these moments of surrender were a coming home to myself: being a priest was simply an expression of my truest identity. It wasn't the end-point, or an ambition in itself, but a vehicle that I sensed would be liberating; letting me maybe lose and probably find myself in something much bigger than me.

Fears of frumpy spinsterhood lost their grip as I stopped wrestling with the image of a vicar in my head and said Yes to life instead. Yes to this way that would allow me to speak to people of a God who brings us home to ourselves. A God who gently unearths our deepest identity from the crustation of pretence and illusions we try to keep in place. I wanted to be part of something that says Yes to all the bruised, broken, flawed bits of our humanity and clothes those vulnerabilities in love, not in rejection and judgement. I wanted to be part of a church that wasn't stuck in the respectability of Sunday services but went out and affirmed the creativity of God in the whole of life, not just in the bits that got labelled holy.

I stayed in chapel a long time after Compline was finished and the candles had been blown out. In a little corner of the wall behind the altar was the light of a candle that was never extinguished; it carried on flickering as I finally got up to leave and climb the stairs to the attic floor where I was now staying.

At the top of the house, down the long corridor leading to the sisters' rooms, I noticed all the trays of nettles, herbs and plants that Novice Joy was growing along the windowsill. She called it her apothecary. I called it her nettle farm. It looked like the enthusiastic hobby of a nursery school child whose appetite for home-grown cress had given way to the need for more hardcore flavours.

Catching her tending these nettles one afternoon I had asked her what they were for. She had told me these plants were ingredients that she mixed up as herbal remedies to heal her inflamed and blemished skin. I hadn't thought much more of it except to ask if they worked. I hadn't anticipated their significance.

"Well they're for my skin you see. It's becoming so problematic."

Which made it undiplomatic to look directly at her skin and see what she was talking about – but I couldn't help myself. I had never noticed that Novice Joy had suffered from acne, only that she had the most exquisitely defined jawbone.

"Every now and then my skin just flares up and my stomach bloats horribly and I can feel this tension in my tummy … Sometimes I just can't bear to touch or look at my face … I can't bear it. I don't want anyone looking at me; I don't want anybody to see me. I know it's a stress thing … but I feel by doing this I'm finding a creative response, being part of the healing."

I had watched as she peered, almost pleadingly, at the herbs and briefly patted the girdle that hung around the grey tunic cloaking her.

Now as I walked past the rows of foliage on my way to bed I thought about her and her search for wholeness again. In my room I tore out a piece of notepaper and scrawled across it:

Joy! Need to talk about nettles and healing. Want to do some stealth talking in the raspberry patch tomorrow a.m.?

I pushed it under her door.

Tucked into my book at the breakfast table the next morning was a note.

Sure! How about stealth nettle farming on top floor this afternoon? 2 p.m.

The top floor was clear of inhabitants at that time of day and we talked freely. Joy introduced me to the herbs and their healing properties and again I asked, "But do they work?", hastily adding that they certainly seemed to have done so.

"Well, I think they help. I think they calm the inflammation for sure."

"I loved what you said before about growing these to participate in your healing."

"Yes, I think that's it. They definitely do have a physiological effect but there's also something about getting back to my body that is so important for me."

I could see the capital letters forming the question in my mind: WHY? I THOUGHT NUNS WERE ABOUT TRANSCENDING THEIR BODIES?

But I stayed quiet in the hope that she would say more.

"I think this inflammation and tension, or whatever it is, is my body's way of telling me something's wrong … that I'm stuck up here in my mind. So much of what we're about here is to do with prayers and words and spirit. We're saturated in it, to be honest. It feels like a struggle for me to be in touch with my physical energy; to be at home and whole within my body too."

Her face wrinkled up into the gentlest frown but she smiled as she spoke, as if she knew how ridiculous it was for a contemplative nun to be frustrated by all the praying she had to do.

"What bothers you most? I mean, is it the celibacy?" I had to ask.

"No, no, that feels very life-giving still." She paused and touched the skin around her jaw as she pondered.

"No, I think it's the feeling of unwholeness with my body, I find it so hard to accept my body and that shows itself in my relationship with food and then my skin … my skin flares up horribly and, oh I don't know, it's so silly that I care."

She began to laugh off her words as if they contained too much nonsense, but I wasn't about to let her walk away from this internal wrestling match; I needed to know all about it.

"Then I guess the nettles are immensely healing ... they remind you that you do care and that your body is important ... that you are prepared to listen to it."

Joy nodded as she continued, "You know, recently I've begun just putting my hands on my chin and on my stomach as a way of making peace with myself, like I am almost affirming and blessing the part of me that is so sore and unacceptable ..."

I thought of my photograph, the picture of my fourteen-year-old self, that I kept with me in my own small healing ritual.

"And in breathing too; meditating and focusing on my breath – that has become such a vital way of feeling whole again. Did you know that there's a Hebrew tradition where they believe that just breathing is saying the name of God? As if it's our most primal prayer and humans have been designed to say it and live by it: just breathing the name of God."

"That is so beautiful." I thought about the years I'd spent contriving together the right religious buzzwords to make the most impressive and right-on prayers, and I felt drained. Yet Joy hadn't had anything like this in her background and I was intrigued by what experiences might have brought her here.

"Where do you think this dis-ease comes from? I mean, it's not like you are surrounded by copies of *Hello* and repeats of Beverley Hills 90210 ... so what is it? How can it be that even here in a Welsh convent women can still feel they are not right in their own bodies?"

She laughed at the impossibility of it. "I know, you'd think this would be the one place we women could come and feel all right. But it's no escape ... it just makes these realities more felt."

"Even nuns seem to follow in Eve's footsteps. It seems to be mapped out for us just like it was for her: that being a woman and all that that entails is painful and vulnerable, even if it's life-giving! We can't escape it – not even here. One way or another all of us get tangled in the same story; whether it's fawning subservience or not loving our bodies or hiding our authentic self for the sake of other people's good opinion."

Novice Joy's eyebrows were raised in recognition.

"I mean, men have their own stuff too. But women – well, it doesn't matter if we're nuns, or mothers, or eight, or seventy-eight ..."

She finished my sentence: "... the Eden story repeats itself in so many ways and lives."

There was quiet between us for a moment.

"You know what I'm beginning to think?" I leant back against the window, unfolding my arms and resting back on them. "I think that when we trip over these inequalities and injustices and inauthenticities it's a wake-up call; our chance to see that it wasn't meant to be like this. These things are our reminder to get up, to name what's fragmented and twisted, and begin looking in new places for wholeness – with ourselves and with each other."

Joy nodded briskly. "Yes, I think you're right ... it's like Julian of Norwich said, 'There's our fall and there's the recovery from the fall, and both are the mercy of God.'"

I thought about my falls and scrapes: the religion, the efforts, the bids for control and perfection, the judgements and the pretences. How they had wracked me, and how I, in turn, had hurt others with them too. And looking back across the years I began to see how this trail of fig leaves and fractured things became part of the call; drawing me on in search of healing, reunion and love.

27

Ground E

It's one thing to surrender yourself to the silence and love when they are surrounding you. It is something else to hold that silence and love within you when you leave and make your way back into a noisy, demanding world. Part of me felt sad that I couldn't quite crowbar myself into a vocation to the religious life; after all, these women, and the men who lived and worked alongside them, were managing to live with the kind of mutuality and equality one might dream of. Nobody told these women that they couldn't lead or teach or drive tractors and farm the land, or that they should get married and have babies because that's the way it is for women. Ty Mawr was at least one place on earth in which I could see women and men being partners in making something good and truthful flourish; something beyond their own personal agendas. It was a snapshot of pre-Fall Eden, post-Fall.

But no matter how much I tried to envisage myself in the grey tunic of a novice sister, I couldn't push aside this knowing, this seeing myself as a priest somewhere else. I didn't know where that somewhere else would be, only that it wasn't going to be a geographical parish so much as a cultural one. At my selection interviews I attempted to make sense of it; at college I tried to explain it to my tutors; and eventually I had to face my Bishop and claw back some theological gravitas on hearing myself utter the words "I want to be a vicar but not in a church." He peered at me over his spectacles. That was not the way to talk about being a priest. Only I couldn't say anything clearer, I couldn't sum it up because I couldn't yet see it.

I poured out the story of the fearful God of my childhood and how my Dad had come through for me, helping to unburden that tyranny from me. I described my failures, from my short-lived attempt at nursing to fears that my life would be less than it could be if I had a dog-collar round my neck. I talked about Joe and the guilt I felt about not having been there for him in the end; and about the convent and its silence and the things it revealed and healed. And from this heap of unfinished stories the Church discerned that I did have a vocation. I was sent to Cambridge for another two years of theological training and told to listen carefully for where God was calling me.

I knew how to listen. I had done it at the convent, free-falling in trust that the answers would emerge in their own time.

But that didn't stop me trying to short-circuit the waiting time with some good suggestions of my own. I wanted to know. I wanted to see right now what this future would look like. I wanted to be in control and make it happen.

Nun was off the list.

What about chaplain? That's being a priest but not in a church.

Schools, hospitals, prisons … they all have chaplains. Maybe I was going to be a hospital chaplain and redeem my earlier experiences. My monkey mind jumped and shouted and grabbed hold of possibilities to fill the emptiness. I grew impatient and doubtful and tried to fill the waiting time with answers of my own design rather than letting the right thing emerge and become what it would be.

Then something did emerge. On a freezing cold night in Cambridge as I walked back to my college came a phone call from a friend working in bioethics. "I've got the recent abortion statistics in front of me and I had to tell you … it says that an abortion took place at 28 weeks because of a bilateral cleft lip and palate: that's what you had, isn't it?"

It wasn't what I'd had, but the surgical reconstruction I had undergone is the same as that performed on young adults with a cleft palate. I quickly did the maths: 28 weeks gestation … that's about seven months. Babies are born at less than that and can survive.

"A cleft lip and palate – are you sure?"

Could that seriously be a reason to terminate? I didn't know exactly where the law stood. I was only aware that Down's syndrome is the most common reason for terminating a pregnancy on the grounds of abnormality. It was something that I shuddered to contemplate. But a cleft lip and palate wasn't the same; children at my church, two of my teachers, a friend's father; we all know people who have this condition and have had it corrected. How could it be possible to make this grounds for an abortion?

I checked the Office for National Statistics and saw that there had been nine other abortions, also for cleft lip and palate. I rang my friend back. "There wasn't just one, there were nine others."

"Yes, but that single case I told you about was after 24 weeks."

"At 28 weeks."

"Exactly; that one is legal under Ground E of the Abortion Act."

I went back and read up on Ground E and how an amendment to the 1967 Abortion Act had come into effect in 1991 to allow abortion up to and including birth *where there is a substantial risk that if the child were born it would suffer from such physical or mental abnormalities as to be seriously handicapped.*

Another call to my friend: "Are you sure it was for a cleft lip and palate? Were there other reasons do you think?"

"That's the recorded reason, but I think it would be worth us doing some digging, Joanna."

So we dug. I spoke to a solicitor, the brother of a team leader at Good News Crusade, who specialized in disability and children's rights. He was stunned at the possibility this might have happened, not just once but ten times in one year. "It's very interesting, Joanna. In 1990, when the debate over this law was taking place, two lawyers warned of the risk that, if the amendment passed, conditions like cleft palate and club foot might become grounds for abortion. Lord Steel and Harriet Harman MP were outraged at their scare-mongering and recommended these lawyers be reported to the Bar Council for suggesting such discreditable things. Now it seems they are happening."

Good. Someone else wanted to dig as well.

"I think we should inform the police, let them know there's evidence of a potential abuse of the law here."

"Whooaaaa … the police?"

"Look, Joanna, are you up for this?"

Even if I had known then what "this" would eventually become, it would have been very difficult to weigh up whether it would be worth it. I couldn't have known how it would turn my life upside down; how it would affect my family, my future and, not least, reach the unknown woman who had gone through this abortion who, I would find out ten years later, had been under huge pressure to terminate this pregnancy. Nor would I ever know the lives and decisions it would help to change. All I knew at that point was that I was in a unique position to push for accountability: were we really a society who condoned the termination of viable human life on the grounds of such defects and flaws? Working so hard to bring about diversity and equal opportunities in every system, every network and community of our country; trying to change attitudes towards people with disabilities; removing barriers to flourishing, especially for those with physical and mental challenges: it all seemed to fall flat if we justified the termination of certain lives on the very grounds we wanted to accept.

I thought about Ali and me and the slurs and abuse we had encountered as children; was abortion really the best that we, as reasonably evolved human beings, could come up with in response to that suffering? That it might have been better for us not to have existed than to have experienced the cruelty and ignorance of others? It seemed to be a systematic, legalized slump into fear and doubt about the value of certain lives.

I began to reach out and ask questions. I found that governments had already started asking questions like this from an economic perspective. Questions that they addressed to mathematicians and geneticists. Questions like, *If we started screening every pregnant woman, not just those over 32, for foetal disability then how much would it cost us versus how much it costs the State to care for disabled children should they be undetected and born?* And I found out that the mathematicians answered Yes, it is economically effective to screen every pregnant woman and offer terminations where necessary. It will save taxpayer money. I thought of Alastair and all the NVQs in Hotel and Catering he'd achieved. I thought of him now in his workspace at Dundries Nurseries, the country's number one videotape recycler: methodically working through a pile of 12,000 videotapes, taking apart their nineteen component pieces and saving the landfill from the careless disposal of unwanted plastic. Maybe mathematicians and geneticists were the wrong people to be making these life or death calculations. It seemed the weighing up of human life in the scales of tax bills and medical prognosis was leading to the disposal of lives – lives that would have meaning and make a contribution to our society if we were willing to acknowledge it.

There was something inhumane about needing to demonstrate a person's ultimate worth in terms of their contribution to the national GDP. And it overlooked the fact that, unless we are victims of a sudden tragedy, as we age we all become disabled in one way or another and have to adjust to the inconvenience and dependence and limitations it brings about. How do we prepare and rise to the challenges of disability if we make abortion on the grounds of disability a justifiable matter of course?

I began having conversations with friends, and friends of friends. People told me how they were offered an abortion because their baby was found to have missing fingers. Another man got in touch to tell me how his mother was offered an abortion because he had been diagnosed with a club foot. My friend who had started all this arranged for me to meet a cleft palate surgeon. He talked candidly and sadly about mothers who came to him from other hospitals having been alarmed and urged to consider terminating their babies with a cleft palate diagnosis; mothers desperate for a second opinion. Mothers expecting a much-wanted baby who had now been turned into bioethicists by doctors who warned them how disfigured their child would be, and how near or far someone would have to stand from their child before seeing there was something wrong.

I knew something of what that could be like, perhaps not as acutely, not entirely the same. But I had been that spurned child and I had also been through the same surgery. I had a voice and I wanted to use it where others had been silenced. We began to push for answers. Paul, my solicitor, set the process in motion; nothing more than a paper trail winding its way slowly through one police in-tray after another. And life at college carried on moving steadily towards the date of my ordination.

28

Valentine Message

In the Church of England the newly ordained first become curates, charged with 'the cure of souls' among other more down-to-earth tasks. It is an apprenticeship for the priesthood completed under the training and leadership of an experienced vicar. Most of the students in my year had got their curacies sorted out but a handful of us were still poring over the Curacy Job File that sat in the porter's lodge and was updated with new vacancies each week.

Jane Addis was by now living in Chester, as was Rosalind, and so in the New Year I trekked up-country to visit them. On the Sunday morning, the three of us wandered around Chester Cathedral. Its stained glass windows were stunning and hopeful even in the wan light of January and, thinking how much the warm stone reminded me of Ty Mawr, I remarked that I would love to be ordained in a cathedral like this. Which is sometimes how God sets us up because six weeks later an unexpected curacy was advertised in the Curacy Job File. It was based in Chester, in the neighbouring parish to Jane's.

The vicar advertising this curacy was Bob, a Scouser with a voice that boomed hymns and a laugh that rocked the earth on which he stood. His wisdom was just as deep and as resonant. I went up for a couple of weekends to meet Bob and his churchwardens and to visit the church incognito. It was a large thriving parish engaging with every imaginable aspect of the wider community. I told Bob that this was the place for me and to my relief he agreed. It was in the course of these discussions and meetings that I mentioned the legal action that I had begun.

"The police have investigated – very superficially – and have told us the abortion forms were filled in correctly … which obviously completely misses the point. Paul, my solicitor, is looking for us to go to the High Court for a judicial review. So although it's all gone quiet at the moment it will resurface later this year, probably after my ordination."

Bob nodded and stroked his beard thoughtfully.

"Well, you've got that ball rolling. So whenever it does come up we will deal with it and make sure the right support is in place for you."

That was good. It was good to be heading to a church with a vicar who would be supportive.

Now that there was a curacy to look forward to and a church full of people to meet it seemed like a good time to begin dealing with the need for a new wardrobe of post-student clothes that I could work around the impending clerical collar. My big red trainers had been the subject of a polite email from the College Principal who, despite having enjoyed my sermon, questioned the appropriateness of such footwear poking out from under my alb. The end of red trainers was nigh; I needed to work out how to relinquish them and take on a dog collar and still feel like me underneath it all. On Valentine's Day – without a Valentine in sight – I headed down to London, making a beeline for the Kings Road, my favourite London haunt.

Back when I was at Trinity College, word had circulated that the women in the year above me had gone out and bought red silk lingerie to wear under their garb on the day of their ordination; I guessed they wanted to make sure they still had faith in their womanhood. Now, faced with the prospect of all those black and white robes and sensible shoes, I could see where they were coming from; perhaps swapping red trainers for red silk undies was an upgrade becoming of a newly professional young woman.

But in all honesty it wasn't my knickers that were bothering me. The problem was that anything I chose had to be worked around that most unflattering of things: the clerical shirt. It was difficult to know how I could ever manage to make that shapeless garment, buttoned-up to some halfhearted height at one's throat, look even vaguely nice. I had been measured for my shirts by visiting clerical tailors and had duly placed my orders, only to be dismayed when the shirts arrived with two inches added on to all my measurements. "Yes, they do that to the smaller women's shirts, I think it might be a modesty thing", a size 8 ordinand commiserated with me. I had been called to the priesthood and sentenced to life wearing a polycotton sack, I thought begrudgingly. Even the Kings Road was letting me down. Every suit I tried on rucked up over the excess of ugly black fabric and I made up my mind to send the shirts back with a strongly worded letter. Which is why, amidst these vexatious musings, my attention was caught by the long hoardings running the length of the pavement: LONDON FASHION WEEK 2003 LONDON FASHION WEEK 2003 LONDON FASHION WEEK 2003. The words followed me down Duke of York Square until I got the message: the fashion industry. Where was God in the fashion industry?

On that particular day it felt like He was nowhere to be found. Where was God when I needed help channeling spiritual gravitas with all the sassiness of Carrie Bradshaw hitting 5th Avenue? And that was just *my* niche problem; what about all those women and girls and men who every day searched their wardrobe in despair for something to wear that didn't make them hate themselves; or all those people who, despite all the real stresses and problems in their life, just wished that for once they could look good in their clothes and not slightly inadequate. Because, for all our dismissal of fashion as frivolity, somehow these things still seem to get to us and matter to us.

I thought about the God I worshipped: the God who wraps the light around Himself like a garment, who designed the cosmos with awesome playfulness and precision – just because. The God who spoke human life into being and kept pursuing that creative vision until man and woman existed together as equal vital partners. The God who delighted in telling them that they were going to be living, breathing reflections of divine creativity. When did we name and celebrate this bit of the God story? That creativity and design are part of our spiritual DNA; a God-given gift and vocation.

In ancient times God had instructed the ancient priestly garments to be designed in gold and blue and purple and scarlet and fine linen. Now we had black polycotton and a guilty relationship with clothes, torn by suspicion, longing and a super-spiritual belief that material temptations were to be shunned in the name of God. I thought back to the complete delight I took in my dresses as a tiny child: the patterns, the feel of the fabric and the way I could make them swirl out around me if I spun round really fast. I remembered too how much I'd hated the brown flares Mum had made me wear as an eight-year-old, and my attempts to paperclip the flare back into a neat taper round my ankle. I thought about how my enjoyment of clothes had given way to shame and awkwardness in my teens, and the way I had become a silent spectator of those who still got pleasure out of dressing up. I remembered the wistful ache when, aged seventeen, Jess had unpacked her make-up case and held up a crimson coloured lipstick to me and asked, "Don't you just have days when only *red* lipstick will do?"

Sitting on a bench near Sloane Square watching the flurry of cold shoppers, I thought about God and where He was to be found in our search for the elusive perfect outfit. No matter how much part of my brain just laughed and scoffed at the idea of God taking seriously the sartorial angst of Western consumers, part of me suspected that that belief was rotten; a superficial dismissal of some deeply skewed wounds. And what about all the environmental and economic exploitations for which our consumerist appetites would have to answer? We could try and deny the place of clothes and all that stuff but we all have a relationship with them, just like we have a relationship with the English language or whichever language we speak. Because these tools are a way in which we speak and present ourselves to the world. They are part of how we tell the story of who we are, what we believe in, what values we have and who we want to reveal ourselves to be.

For years Alastair had been dressed in hand-me-down clothes, none of which really fitted him, until on a trip to the States I started buying Abercrombie & Fitch shirts for him – in the correct size. Suddenly he sensed the transformation: "I'm a handsome man", he said, smiling in the mirror. And he was. Now his shirts clothed him and made him look sharp. Now that his shirts fitted he wanted a smart blazer and sunglasses to go with them. He wanted his hair styled in a particular way. And so his new clothes began to speak differently; they revealed his handsomeness and his confidence, eradicating the message of oversized seconds which told the world he wasn't worth buying new clothes for because he was disabled and didn't really matter.

The truth is that clothes, design, fashion and style do matter: they are part of what makes us human. They are spun from our spiritual DNA; gifts of creativity to enjoy and inspire, whether you're a small child, a twenty-something nun, a young man wanting to be known for more than a disability, a celebrity or a woman on the verge of ordination to the priesthood.

And if these things matter to us and impact us for good or ill, then the Church should speak of God in this industry. Which is how, that Valentine's Day, an idea was born, to some day start a chaplaincy in fashion.

29

St Bob, Patron Saint of Curates

On 6 July 2003 I was ordained a deacon and the seed that had been sown and taken a long time to germinate was at last coming into bloom – even though I was dressed in black and white. My new parishioners decorated my house and threw a welcome party and listened with encouraging smiles as I preached my first sermon. And, as word got out that I was a lousy cook, so the invitations began arriving: *'We'd love to get to know you better – come for supper!'*

These people became family; we ate, drank and prayed together. And we were passionate about not remaining holed-up in a church building but getting involved in the strained, ugly, hard-bitten edges of leafy suburban Chester. A group began a tiny mission congregation based in a nearby school, reaching out to families and the elderly; we started a café and credit union on the social housing estate in the middle of the parish, I worked there every Tuesday trying to improve my cooking skills, but chatting with customers remained my strong point.

It was like Emmanuel Church all over again, except my childish distinctions between Us and Them had now blurred. There were no longer the do-gooders and the poor recipients of that good. It was a community of people prepared to be open to their own failings and fallibility as much as a place where hope was offered to those who were struggling and reluctant to enter our church building. It was the kind of place I needed to be; making my home among those outside church as much as taking my place behind the altar inside it. I found myself watching people now, pondering how they reflected sparks of God in their own unique way. It might be buried deep beneath a lot of horrid life experiences but, in the spaces in which I sat with people who were bereaved, guilty, abused, flailing, trying, desiring or depressed, I waited in silence, letting people tell their stories; letting that divine image begin to show through, even in glimmers.

Bob, my training vicar, led me through each new task, sacrament and encounter without hurry, talking through the questions I needed to be asking of myself, and those that might help others find release from their various prisons. He gently wrestled away my carefully crafted sermon scripts, launching me into the spontaneity of sermons preached roving around the dais instead of gripping the lectern. He refused to let me get too comfortable in middle-class churchy concerns and ushered me into the chaotic parts of the parish where people looked for stability and shelter rather than sound preaching. And, despite being the leader of a busy, noisy, evangelical, chorus-singing congregation, Bob allowed me to introduce them to unfamiliar things like silence and contemplation and even the foreign waft of incense.

Four months after my ordination we prayed for him and his wife and sent them off to Pakistan where they were to visit a missionary from our church. I can't remember the exact phrase he used before he left. Was it "While the vicar's away the curate will play"? Was it "Don't get up to too many pranks"? Whatever he joked, neither of us expected the scene of satellite vans, television crews and spilling mailbags at St Michael's that he would find on his return several weeks later.

Just days after Bob and Pam had departed, my solicitor called to say we were on: *'expect to appear at the High Court within the next four weeks; and make sure you've got some people with you to support you on the day.'* I called my Dad and my Aunt Helen and asked them if they would come with me. It was all beginning to feel a long way from a number on the abortion statistics and that phone call in Cambridge the year before. There were warning flashes of the rumbles that lay ahead: journalists began to get in touch and ask for interviews. My three phones rang. Constantly. Besieged by press, I couldn't get out to buy food and was so grateful to a photographer who slipped out to buy me some milk and supplies. The Bishop called me in for a conversation and sent me off to Diocesan House for some emergency media training. The Diocesan Press Officer, David, arranged for the entire staff of Church House to wait outside for me and impersonate a High Court press scrum; then sent me out to meet them with a prepared statement, once as if I had won the right to a judicial review, and then a second time as if I had lost.

The date for court was set for Monday 1 December, and on Friday 28 November Paul handed the case over to a brilliant and renowned barrister, Richard Gordon QC, and the ante seemed to have been upped once again. On Sunday 30 November the BBC sent a correspondent to Chester to film me making the journey down to London and capture the human story behind the unfolding legal case. Thankfully that correspondent had been a good friend of mine at Cambridge, and his presence as a friend reassured me where his presence as a journalist unnerved me. It began to cross my mind that we might actually put up a worthy fight in court even if we were never going to win a judicial review. But a good fight was something – at least it would break into the stalemate that the public discussion had become.

Abortion always felt like a distasteful subject for debate, whether among friends or at parliamentary level. It was a vote-loser and MPs would rather spend hundreds of hours discussing fox-hunting than discrimination against the unborn. There was little political appetite for returning it to the House for fresh debate, even in the light of new advances in medical technology; even though a 4D screening could now show foetal development and leave people in no doubt about the fact that these were viable babies at risk.

Thirty-six years after the Abortion Act had been introduced, it seemed that the debate hadn't moved on much, and came down to the two sides hurling slogans past each other: "*A woman's right to choose*" versus "*Abortion is murder*". There wasn't much space for listening; to do so might threaten the hard-won rights of the sisterhood and nobody really wanted to do that. When it was put like that, *I* didn't really want to do that. I knew that in a messy world there were going to be times when abortion was the choice to make. Only I had stumbled on another story and, unless I told it, it might not be heard. That was why I brought the case: because it would give me an opportunity to tell a different story; not just to bring about a national debate, but to voice another story to all those women who were, and who ever would find themselves, faced with a doctor and the news that their unborn baby had some kind of definable flaw and that their best hope would be to abort. I wanted to stand for something else, something beyond the end of the story that doctors might tell.

Because doctors, whichever point of view they hold, can only paint a picture for a mother and father in clinical terms. They might be able to say "your child will never walk" or "by the time they are eighteen they will have undergone this many operations" or "people will recognize your child by what's wrong with them". But neither doctors nor anyone else can tell a mother and father the full picture: the real layers of meaning that their child's life will have; the sense of achievement when they outgrow expectations, or demonstrate staggering courage, or express their love for their parents in their own unique way. Nobody can do that. Doctors might have predicted the difficulties Alastair and I had had, but they couldn't tell Mum and Dad about the relationships, the experiences, the full journey that we would make in living life beyond those painful experiences. Because that is about believing that, although it might not be the life you were anticipating, a life can be made for your child that is more than a medical prognosis. And it's tough because, when you're in that room listening to a medical prognosis, all you're likely to hear is the worry and fears and doubts of your monkey mind yelling that your life is over.

And that's why I wanted to go to the High Court that Monday morning, because I wanted to tell those mothers and fathers and doctors and opponents a different reality; one that might exist beyond their worst fears and a medical diagnosis.

* * *

On Monday 1 December, after several rounds of breakfast TV interviews, Paul, Dad, Helen and I gathered in Richard Gordon's chambers around the corner from the High Court. I was heartened by Richard's confidence and the insight with which he had reworked the legal arguments afresh. But all that disappeared as we headed out and I saw the crowd of photographers and journalists, television crews, well-wishers and opponents waiting at the gates across the street. I hadn't even made it across the road before the crowd moved and surrounded me, thrusting cameras, microphones and flashes in my face and shouting urgent questions at me. It was nothing like the jolly mock-up that the Church House staff had put on for me. I tried to smile and keep moving and not tread on a reporter but I generally felt like I was crowd-surfing my way through all these experiences, lurching through a tumble of press interviews and legal proceedings, and all the time trying to hold onto the clarity of my views and the story to which anyone could riposte, "Yeah, but you wouldn't want to make a woman have a baby she didn't want, would you?"

Everyone wanted to know what I wanted or hoped to achieve. Did I want to ban all abortion? Did I want these doctors to be prosecuted? How did I feel about the mother? There were no soundbite answers, so I tried to ask my own questions. Like: Do we want to live in a society where we reject people with disabilities? Do we think that we're going to evolve as human beings and as a society if we try and stamp out suffering instead of gathering together to meet it with shared courage? And where do we stop in trying to rid ourselves of suffering? Because it pretty much comes with the territory of being a human being and our humanity is seen in how we respond to it. Why should one life with identifiable deformity be given no chance when the rest of us with our carefully concealed disabilities get on and live without ever being called out on our flaws?

In the quietness of the courtroom, in front of two judges and squashed up between a Sky News journalist and my aunt came the space for my barrister to put forward the arguments surrounding the case and the law I was hoping to clarify. Was this what the law was put in place for – to allow abortion for conditions like cleft lip and palate? Had the law been abused in this case? Was it in the public interest to allow a judicial review? And did I have standing to bring the case at all?

The judges retired to deliberate and around me the courtroom hummed with journalists trying to read the situation and second-guess the outcome.

A while later the judges returned and the woman from Sky News whispered "Good luck", but within a couple of sentences of Mr Justice Rose's opening comments Paul turned around to me and shook his head, "We haven't done it." I whispered to Helen, "Did you get that already?" I couldn't see anything in what the judge had said to indicate I'd lost. In fact he was saying that if I hadn't brought the case then who would be able to? He was saying that my experience of having undergone bi-maxillary reconstruction and growing up with a brother who has Down's syndrome gave me a unique standing to bring this case to public attention. The judge carried on talking and I carried on trying to see why Paul thought we had lost until Sky News girl whispered "Well done." And I let myself believe that we had actually won. There would be a judicial review of the police's decision not to investigate and take seriously this potential abuse of the Law. There would be a fresh and rigorous look at what Jeremy Paxman described on *Newsnight* later that evening as "a very British hypocrisy".

Outside the High Court I met the maelstrom of press with my statement: the one I'd scribbled for the unlikely event in which I was successfully granted a judicial review. It was a strange feeling, that kind of success, though. It's not the kind that you achieve and own; it was something that I had set in motion with a small group of others and which had now grown and gathered momentum far beyond my possession. Now I had to run to keep up with it: stepping up every time a microphone was pointed at me, letting the story be heard, and the legal arguments be made. If I had lost that day I would have been glad of the opportunity to draw attention to what was happening behind closed doors.

But instead we had been successful and the story turned international. And I wondered if I would have the energy to keep up with all the television and radio interviews that Dad and Helen were busily mapping for the coming hours and following days. By 9pm I had shared most of the evening headlines with news of the start of the trial of Ian Huntley, the Soham child murderer, and, in exhaustion, walked out of my Channel 4 News studio interview with Jon Snow through the wrong door and straight into a broom cupboard. With relief I turned round to find the comedy hadn't been lost on the cameraman and Jon, who met my laughter with a huge grin and thumbs up. If it had happened following an interview with a particular female news anchor earlier that evening I'm pretty sure she would have leapt up to bolt the door behind me. The hostility towards what I was doing from female journalists was sometimes barely concealed, and again and again came their demand to explain why I was attacking a woman's right to choose.

And I got it: I got the injustice that women often relentlessly and systematically suffer at the hands of men. I knew first hand, like many women do in their own particular ways, the inequality, abuse and lack of autonomy and respect that life as a woman can bring, and how this will sometimes lead to the need for safe abortion. But the triumph of feminism seemed to have got stuck there, as if abortion is the best we can do for women – a hard-won political victory that we can't afford to jeopardise even by acknowledging the raw deal it can be for women. I wanted to say, "Hold on … is this as far as we go? Is this what we're settling for?" For all the problems abortion might do away with, it too is a violence that the woman undergoes. Can't we hope for something better?

My friends who'd had abortions had all had a horrible time; none of them were whooping hoorays over their right to choose. More often it wasn't a choice so much as the only way that they were offered by the men in their lives to get out of an impossible situation.

Nothing brought this home to me more than meeting a woman in the waiting room of the obs and gynae consultant I'd gone to see the year before. I hadn't noticed her across the room from me until she started crying. When I went over to give her a tissue she sobbed harder. As if she was relieved to have someone else there.

"Are you by yourself?"

She was.

Then she told me how she was pregnant with twins and one of them had been diagnosed with Down's syndrome. Her husband wanted her to abort the twin with Down's but she didn't want to; she didn't want to risk the life of either twin. Her family was against abortion and told her she'd be on her own if she had one. Her husband told her he would leave if she didn't. Now she was here, alone.

Women being left in an agonizing position, facing terrifying consequences whichever decision they make, doesn't feel like much of a choice at all; it's still women left taking the strain, maybe forced to do something that goes against every instinct they have to protect the unborn life that they're carrying – even though it may be missing a limb or part of its palate, or be chromosomally enhanced, or unlikely to walk. It's not that one decision is easier than another but that the concept of choice has been hijacked by the tellers of one part of the story. It is as if the fear of naming our right to choose *life* and celebrating the strength it takes to do that might be too risky politically and might set back the position of women.

I wanted to find sound bites to express my doubts about the way abortion was being widely normalized in order to make it easier for women to endure. It seemed a short-sighted policy because it might equally let women down, denying them space to acknowledge their loss, and even preventing men and women from becoming a life-giving solution to what seems an inconvenience or an altogether bad prognosis.

But it's tricky to be the one asking the questions when you've got journalists and photographers camped outside your front door. When I returned to Chester and found myself doorstepped by press, I was grateful for parishioners who invited me to the safety of their home tucked away along a private road, who gave me space to formulate careful responses in newspaper articles and to work out what I was going to tell Bob when he returned from Pakistan.

When he did return, to find television camera crews filming the Sunday morning service and St Michael's now the most infamous church in Chester, he couldn't have been more supportive. Deluged by more mail than I could open, Bob arranged for someone to help me open all the letters – and filter the rabidly hateful ones. It didn't always work; one envelope in particular misled me with its comic depiction of an alien in biro next to the address. When I opened it up I found a card with a very definite drawing of Satan himself; underneath were scrawled the words *Jepson you sit at the Devil's feet you evil woman*. I began to see the potential for decorating the walls of my downstairs loo with these letters. Visitors could be lost in there for some considerable time with images and messages like this to read.

Many people decided to cut out – and sometimes cut up – pictures of my face from the newspapers and send them to me with comments. But if this threatened to knock my confidence, a moment of integration came when two people sent me the same picture of myself within a matter of days of each other. One had written in the accompanying letter "the kindness shines through your eyes". The other sender hadn't written a letter at all; she just sent the ripped out page with the same photo on it and underneath had inked her tirade, *you have such a cold face – you should really start letting that smile reach your eyes.*

At this point I'd have expected ghosts of the past to come back; only they didn't. Instead I felt relief, as if I'd suddenly been unhooked from an intravenous drip of reactive and useless commentary that had been feeding me untruths about myself. I lay the two photographs of myself side by side on the dining room table and looked at them. Neither sender would probably ever know who Joanna Jepson was; they were just responding, kindly or unkindly, to a persona. All that this face of the young curate in the newspaper would reflect were their own attitudes and conclusions and hope. Just like the other kids at school had seen. Only now, splashed across the front pages of national newspapers and reviled or feted on internet chat threads, it didn't really matter, because I knew who I was, the doubts and hopes I held and, deep down, what I was about. And that, though it had been a long time coming, was a peace that I could live with.

30

Thursday Morning Crem Rota

Whilst he had given me admin support, prayer support and organized a website in support of my case, Bob did not let me off any preaching duties. Nor, a few weeks later, did he arrange for me to be quietly taken off the Thursday morning crematorium rota. Thursday morning at the crem was set aside for the funerals of foetuses aborted in late stage pregnancy. All the local clergy were asked to take their turn in providing funeral services and pastoral care for the families, but I couldn't believe the timing of my appearance on the rota; of all the clergy, surely I would be the least welcome one to send round to these grieving families.

But Bob would hear none of my arguments about pastoral sensitivity, which was really my attempt to hide behind theological excuses. And he was right not to: occupying headlines and press sound bites was a comfortable place to be compared with sitting alongside grieving parents planning a funeral for a much-wanted baby.

And so, heavy-hearted, I went one by one to the families whose little ones would have a slot on that Thursday morning list of services, hoping that they wouldn't recognize me. And one by one I sat with these shocked, empty-handed couples, listening to them telling me about the tiny life that they had named and how they were going to try and say goodbye before they had ever had the chance to say hello.

On Thursday morning the funeral directors brought a coffin to the crematorium where I waited alone in the vestry, and opening it up they unpacked a collection of tiny white cardboard boxes that weighed almost nothing. I stood looking at the little row of boxes at my feet, each with a small name written on it. Nothing about them big enough to convey the vast grief and loss and love that surrounded each one. Just a flimsy, almost weightless box, placed on the plinth in the chapel, named and held in tears and numb prayers.

And then the words, muttered by a mother leaning over the small grave outside: "I'm so sorry." Her husband pulled her close to him and the words gathered into the fog of sadness along with all the other words and tears and prayers that were said that day. Of course she was sorry, we were all sorry. None of us should have been there in that cemetery that day, least of all this little one. It wasn't meant to be like this, and we all felt traumatized by what was happening.

It was only a while later, when the TV cameras and headlines cleared off after the next big story and I was called to a woman in labour, that I remembered the words of that mother standing over the tiny grave. The woman I was with had gone into labour alone and was hoping that her husband would come in time to greet this fragile life that the doctors had said was incompatible with life. The baby girl wouldn't survive and I wondered at how this mother had the strength to go through labour knowing this.

Hours later I sat listening to the mother and father talking about hope and about how, even under the shadow of the words "incompatible with life", they had wanted to let life take its course and have whatever time they could with their newborn. She hadn't survived long enough for me even to baptize her. Instead the family gathered to say goodbye: a father comforting his wide-eyed older sons and an exhausted, stricken mother handing the tiny body covered in vernix and swaddling over to me to hold, and name, and bless. And while I'm praying desperately that I won't be sick because it's all got so hot and smelly in the room, these incredible parents talk about how thankful they are that they were able to meet their daughter and were given a few minutes to hold this loved new life in their arms.

Is this the suffering that doctors want their patients to be able to avoid? The vomit, the mess, the disappointment and the futile exhaustion, the tiny weight of a loved baby in your arms? Is it the tangibility of this grief that doctors want to enable women to avoid by offering terminations? Or are the healing possibilities of those moments that *are* compatible with life overlooked by medics who hope to help women avoid walking in the shadow of death for any longer than they have to? Because that night I saw the extraordinary strength and joy that life – even a few moments of life – brought; and grief clothed by gratitude instead of guilt.

31

A Holy Place in the World

There's something subversive that happens at the end of makeover programmes like Trinny and Susannah. It's that bit when they pull the sheet off the mirror and the woman who has been undergoing the Trinny and Susannah treatment gets to see herself transformed: all newly clothed, made-up and glowing. That bit when the woman starts to cry. It's so intriguing because these programmes are meant to be light-hearted reality entertainment about shopping and shoes, where we all enjoy the fond bossiness with which Trinny and Susannah prey on their subjects, and we smugly watch a public rummage through these women's wardrobes and the ruthless cull with which they empty them. But in the end, after all the bin-bags of hideous, ill-fitting clothes have been filled, we get to the best bit: the part where the woman sees herself in the mirror. And it's no longer a bit of shallow entertainment because you can see that something very moving is happening to that woman.

It's as if that woman is seeing herself afresh; that she isn't just thinking "what a lovely suit they've put me in", but that she sees herself – for the first time in a long time – as someone beautiful and worth dressing and making lovely and bringing out the best in. Because usually the women who cry are the ones who start off the programme looking most in need of some attention; the ones who arrive with little memory of themselves as noticeable, beautiful, special and dignified. So these outward symbols of dignity and worth matter because somehow they also speak truth about the person within: that they matter and are important and have value. It's like a sacramental moment where clothes become the sign of our inner humanity and dignity.

It was an idea that some people around me were almost laughing in disbelief over. "Joanna, the fashion world is just full of narcissists – why don't you go and work with people who really need it?" But I couldn't shake off the desire to pursue the idea and, as I moved to set up a new chaplaincy within the London College of Fashion, I heard another story that broke like unexpected light onto my preparations. It was the story of an officer who was part of the Allied operation to clear and liberate Bergen-Belsen concentration camp. What Lt Col Gonin had found there was total horror:

… corpses piled high or just lying alone where they'd dropped dead; the living scoured by dysentery; people choking on their vomit because they were too weak to turn over. One had to learn to restrain oneself from going to their assistance. One had to get used early to the idea that the individual did not count. One knew that five hundred a day were dying and that five hundred a day would go on dying for weeks before anything we could do would have the slightest effect.

So it might have seemed like a sick joke when the British Red Cross turned up with boxes of red lipstick. Seriously. Of all the medical kits and medicine, blankets and food, toiletry supplies and clean water that they were crying out for – they get red lippy. If I'd opened those boxes up I would have been too appalled by the obvious mistake to have started actually handing it out. But for some reason the lipsticks were distributed and a flabbergasted Lt Col Gonin wrote of what happened:

I wish so much that I could discover who did it, it was the action of genius, sheer unadulterated brilliance. I believe nothing did more for those internees than the lipstick. Women lay in bed with no sheets and no nightie but with scarlet red lips, you saw them wandering about with nothing but a blanket over their shoulders, but with scarlet red lips. I saw a woman dead on the post-mortem table and clutched in her hand was a piece of lipstick. At last someone had done something to make them individuals again, they were someone, no longer merely the number tattooed on the arm. At last they could take an interest in their appearance. That lipstick started to give them back their humanity.

They were recognized as someone once again. That was what the crazy gift of lipstick gave to the walking dead in a concentration camp. And that's the gift that lipstick, clothes, shoes, dresses, suits, scarves, ties, hats and everything else we can design in the name of fashion can give us.

Which is why, when columnists scorned my new role at the London College of Fashion, I could laugh it off and carry on.

This weekend it was revealed that His plan for Joanna has seen her leave her parish to take up a position as chaplain for the London College of Fashion, where she will no doubt be drawn into important debates as to how a benevolent God could permit suffering or the latest Roberto Cavalli collection.[1]

One can see that there is more to the business than mere clothes – there's the cocaine, the parties and the sex for a start – but when Dr Corner, head of LCF, suggests that it is, above all, about feeling good, and that spirituality should play its part, she loses me.[2]

---

[1] Marina Hyde, *Guardian*, Comment is Free, Tuesday 18 July 2006.
[2] Terence Blacker, *Independent*, Tuesday 18 July 2006.

Because comments like this were amusing, and it was true – I was an easy hit for the columnists that week. But, underneath all the quips, I couldn't get over the power fashion has to help us express our integrity or to fracture it, tormenting us or allowing us to feel at home with ourselves.

The problem is, how do we find ourselves on the right side of that divide? When the images of woman that we are given to emulate are so thin and angular; so, frankly, alien to most of us. Most of us don't look like walking coat-hangers – which is basically what a catwalk model is employed to be – and so a lot of the time we don't look as the advertisers and magazines lead us to think we should look when we slip, or rather squeeze, into their sublime clothes. And it taunts us and tells us that our bodies are not quite right; that we look awful, that we're inadequate. Which unfortunately is part of the game, the game that gets us chasing the dream that one day, if we just keep trying and looking hard enough, we will find the clothes that make us look good and make us feel better about ourselves.

As Lent approached one year I sat sharing a chocolate-brownie-and-popcorn-flavoured sundae with one of my parishioners while we discussed what to give up. Chocolate and alcohol have never been the real obstacles to spiritual clarity for me, but shopping or, rather, consumerism has. So I outlined to her my Lenten deal to give up shopping – complete with small print whereby I would still be allowed to purchase essential toiletries and gifts and even new shoes if I managed to get a hole in my present ones. My friend listened and didn't say or eat anything until I'd finished. I was telling her this because I needed there to be just one person, besides God, who would know the official parameters of my Lenten sacrifice and who wouldn't let me wriggle out with some new loophole that allowed me to go shopping five days after Ash Wednesday.

But instead of wagging her chocolatey spoon at me and making it clear that it would be thoroughly shameful if a vicar let down her parishioners by breaking her Lenten fast she just said, "Damn. That's it. That's what I've got to do now." She was annoyed with me for having even mentioned the idea because, she went on, "I trawl the shops, every week, for that one thing; that one item of clothing or accessory that will complete my wardrobe ... And complete me. So that's it: I have to give up shopping for Lent now too."

So for the next six weeks we did our best to stay away from shops and temptation and allow our restless cravings for a bit of retail therapy to be felt. It was like being back at the convent in those frequent moments where I just wanted to kidnap a guest from the retreat house and guzzle all their nice, non-convent-made food and talk all night as a distraction from the circular whir of my unholy daydreams.

Because that's what Lent is for: to give us space to recognize and really feel, very uncomfortably, just how addicted we are to things that will never actually complete and satisfy us. Human beings are experts at taking any of life's random good things and turning them into a blind compulsion. But on a cultural level there's definitely some ironing out to be done in our relationship with shopping, consumerism, fashion and beauty products. These are our easy idols.

When I arrived at the London College of Fashion I discovered that the students there were not the godless, hedonistic, absurd and vacuous creatures people had predicted they would be. That was the noticeable thing: that below the College on Oxford Street roamed girls who all conformed to some kind of uniform – skinny jeans, deconstructed T-shirt, ballet pumps, iron-straight hair – all searching for that great new item of clothing that might make them cooler or more acceptable. Yet the corridors and studios of the College above were filled with people who had no interest in looking exactly the same as anyone else. If I felt at all grim having to wear a clerical collar around the College, that soon gave way to relief that it would just be taken for a very unique fashion accessory. These people were all about pushing stylistic boundaries in order to preserve and expand their artistic integrity; being unique and experimental were just part of that process. Far from being the silly followers of fashion that they are assumed to be, I discovered serious artists in pursuit of beauty, truth and ethical integrity. People who understood the language and nuances of fashion, and how closely that impacts on, and can shape, a person's presence in the world. People who had something very important to offer a hungry audience of young slaves to fashion.

I also saw how your average designer doesn't always get to wrestle fashion's influence away from the strategies of big brands that want to keep us buying fast fashion with no moment to pause and be satisfied. Nor would my students single-handedly avert the debate about size zero models. Because, after all, the advertiser's life's work is to pull us out of ourselves, away from the present moment, with illusions of how perfect life could be if we just had this pair of jeans, or thighs thin enough to put inside the designer jeans. And somewhere in all of this we need to wake up and take responsibility for our part in the game.

Feeling good when we look good in a pair of jeans is great; but it's not a solution that calms the frantic noise telling us we could look like That if we had all This. It never really quietens the drive that compels us to buy more; it doesn't make us content. Because even when we taste the promise of that perfect future – all styled and airbrushed for our consumption – we can't hold it and maintain it. It's an illusion, and if we were able to hold ourselves in the perfection of that moment then economically things would begin to seriously dwindle.

And there's the nub, because, in order to make a profit, industries have to get a hook into our deepest weakness, fear or need. For women, that deepest vulnerability lies in exploiting how we feel about ourselves, in our bodies, our sexuality and our appearance; because this is where we find and express our sense of self in the world. For men it is generally different: men derive their sense of self in the world from the things they gather around themselves – economic power, achievement, success, property – including perhaps their ability to obtain the trophy wife. These external things are the currencies and powers by which men index their place in the world.

But when you're a woman your sense of presence lies in your sexuality and physicality, in the way you carry yourself, the clothes you wear, the looks you give or don't give; in your coy mysteriousness or warm effervescence. Which is why I never really could shake off Rachel Humsley's words that I would be pretty if my teeth were straight. Or why, that night at Bible camp, I'd rather have been pretty than able to speak in tongues. And why, even after three operations to reconstruct my face, I felt crushed when Rich said he preferred long hair on girls.

Because if it's true, as someone once said to me, that "men desire women and women desire men's desire", then that's a pretty pathological system. After all, it's not terribly Girl-Power, which may be why Girl-Power has become such a phenomenon: a way of saying, with a good dose of sass, "We're going to choose not to surrender our need for affirmation to unloving gazes. We're going to grow into the fullness of who we are: celebrating that, instead of constantly comparing ourselves with things we will never be." It's realizing that there's a different place for us to live, and in that place there are no comparisons, because it's *your* place, your holy, unique space; full of gifts and possibility.

It's not a religious space; it's a holy, human space.

Our unique, truthful and irrevocable place in the world.

It is ours.

Nobody else can be us.

People can criticize, reject, mock, attack, dismiss or ignore us but they can never rob us of who we are. Nobody can take from us our way of being. Even when that has been buried a long way under the scars of abuse and trauma. At our core we are each in our own way beautiful, mysterious, gifted; and we are part of something greater than ourselves. That's a truth we wouldn't find so difficult to live if we weren't constantly being set up to compare ourselves with celebrities and each other. That's where shame and pride unsettle us; by making us feel that we have to contrive and earn and prove our worth against another. But we can't be compared with anyone else, because our true value and beauty go beyond the window-dressing by which comparisons are made. And so it is our seeing that needs to be healed and transformed.

But even a preacher-woman wanting to share a message like this might find sermons a dull way to spread the word; it's not the kind of language we speak in the fashion world. Instead I partnered with a photographer, Larry Dunstan, and the charity Changing Faces, and together we put on an exhibition called "Notions of Beauty". Walls of gallery space were given over to Larry's portraits of people revealing, in their various ways, something of their own incomparable beauty, whether a display of strength or of vulnerability. Alastair was invited to sit for a portrait and the studio lights were not fully set up before he had stripped down to his vest and jeans and begun to impersonate some of his screen heroes: David Beckham, Austin Powers and Joey Tribbiani. Leaning against the wall he nonchalantly slipped his hands into his pockets and coolly gazed at the camera with a confidence that could make you weep. He filled the space with his presence. It may have been inspired by Beckham but a roll full of photos later and Alastair owned his particular beauty and integrity. And so did the other sitters: each photograph, detailing the angles, scars, anomalies, twists and expressions of its subject, conveyed people who had discovered how to inhabit their own space in the world. And it was glorious.

But these were rare people who had already met themselves in all their naked reality. What about those who hadn't, those who didn't see that they had a part to play in the flourishing and beauty and healing of the world? Like teenagers who were left alone on Christmas Day with a frozen pizza: twelve- and thirteen-year-olds who were in danger of sexual exploitation; young people who were being passed through the social services system until they had had enough and tried to commit suicide. Children who already believed they were failures because that's the word that hung over their school community.

It was from a school where staff were trying to deal with such things that I was called by the chaplain and asked if the London College of Fashion could do something to help these teenagers see themselves differently. "I want these kids to know that there is hope for them and that they are known and loved by God, even if their families and local government haven't got time for them and the local newspaper keeps putting them down. Will you come and work with us?"

I was there. I took a group of designers who were equally curious and passionate about the power of art and creativity to speak to these children, and we went to visit the school and receive our brief. My students were used to looking at the world and taking their inspiration from anything. Anything. Which is why they were less floored than I was when the chaplain gave us Chapter 1 of

Matthew's Gospel as our starting point. "I want you to bring this to life through fashion."

We stood in a circle looking at the open Bible he'd handed us. It was a family tree but not as artistically organized – more a dense paragraph of ancient, unpronounceable names tracing the lineage of Jesus Christ. "Do we get anything else?" I asked hopefully.

"No, that's your lot. I look forward to seeing what you turn it into." He smiled at us.

One of the designers held the page close up to her face, her eyebrows raised.

"It certainly needs to be turned into *something*."

"Look at these names ... who *are* these people?" another student asked.

It was my turn to take a closer look, but even a childhood of Sunday school classes hadn't familiarized me with the likes of Aminadab, Jotham, Salathiel and Achim. "Why don't we start there then? Let's take this away and begin finding out about these people and get to know their stories."

For the next few weeks my group of volunteers took a few names and rose to the challenge of finding the stuff of catwalk legends buried within this ancient family tree. When we met again there was a mixture of results. One girl didn't turn up at all: the potential for Jehoshaphat, Joram and Uzziah to inspire anything worthy of a twenty-first-century fashionista's talents had quite understandably passed her by. Another student was perplexed by the lack of mothers being given space on the official records and all the credit for this Messiah being taken by the men. She insisted we fill in the blanks and found some more of the women's stories. We all liked that idea. "How about Eve?" I prompted. "Why not use artistic licence and include Eve? Think of all the connections with fast fashion and the environment that we could make."

Jennifer, a second-year surface textiles student, had already honed in on Rahab. "I love that, out of a list of Jesus' male ancestors, two of the women it does include are a prostitute and a victim of injustice who uses prostitution to secure her fair treatment."

Esther, a postgraduate womenswear student, clutched her notebook of reflections on Joseph and Jacob and mused, "Yeah, some of these stories are incredible."

Apparently so. We had prostitution, environmental meltdown, injustice, failure, deceit, sibling-rivalry, exploitation and hope. There seemed to be enough overlap with the lives of pupils in our school to make it come to life.

We also had the narrative of a family tree. Not just the biological family tree that ended with Jesus, but the one that the Gospels nudge us towards; the one that lets people know that there's a spiritual family tree and they're invited to find their place on it. Which is how our collection of outfits was inspired and the Empty Hanger project was born. We returned to the school later that year and invited the pupils to try on the designs we'd created: garments which told the stories of Eve, Jacob, Joseph, Rahab and Jesus and the struggles they'd had to overcome and the part they played in transforming their communities, their people and their world.

At the end of the collection of clothes hung an empty coat-hanger, which we gave the children as an invitation. It was a symbol that we put there to speak of belonging; an invitation to them to begin telling the story of who they are, where they have come from, the battles they have to face, the triumphs they have achieved and the person they are becoming. As pupils worked to design their own outfit, they began to overhear their story and re-tell it, not in the words of disparaging news headlines or the stamp of Ofsted Special Measures but through the encouragement of designers, teachers and a chaplain who enabled them not to dismiss or overlook any of their struggles and failures, because all of their life matters and out of their fiercest battles might come their greatest contribution.

At the end of the workshop a teacher showed me the girl who, having heard the story of Joseph, sewed together the beginnings of her own dream coat imprinted with the words *I dream of being a doctor so I can learn to heal.*

The teacher told us how several members of her family abroad had been caught up in conflict, suffered grave danger and been seriously injured and, as he held her designs up to look at them closely, it was clear that he was moved by her response. "No one is expecting a child from this school to study medicine."

32

Nuns' Tea Party

There are lots of stories we can tell about ourselves, and our story can be told in different ways. The space for reflecting on identity and story and creativity that the Empty Hanger project brought about was something the students from the London College of Fashion were passionate about making possible for disaffected young people. They too began to take inspiration from the stories themselves, incorporating symbols into their coursework and their final collection designs. But I was to have my own opportunity to reflect when the following summer we were asked to run the Empty Hanger project as a summer school for Muslim, Jewish and Christian teenage girls.

I had grown up being told stories about people of other religions. I had absorbed the story preached from the Big Top stage at camp about Muslims rising up to overthrow Christianity, and it had become a part of the story of fear and defensiveness on which my childish imagination had fed. It wasn't the story that I wanted to shape me, and I had done all I could over the years to let go of these stories I'd been told about Muslims. I made a lot of effort and felt pretty self-righteous about the improvements I'd made. That is until I saw a woman in a burka which, since I was living in London, was fairly frequently, and then it got me. It would flare up and the flash of infuriation and offence would leave me feeling totally out of sorts for a while. "*Why don't you get out from under there?*" I railed at them in my mind.

I couldn't tell if I was more peeved at the men who made them wear it, at the women themselves for not refusing or at all those preacher-men who had ever made me feel overruled and suffocated with talk about covering women with male headship. But now I had 30 girls heading my way, a good number of whom were going to be fully veiled: hijabs, niqabs and all. I had seriously to deal with my prejudice, otherwise I was going to feel out of sorts for the whole three days. Only it's hard to go into battle with one's monkey mind and win. And, having learnt in the convent that the more I fight it the louder it shouts, I thought about a more subversive approach. Like, what would I choose to feel towards them instead of vexed suspicion? How would I like my relationship with these women to look?

When the word "sisterhood" popped up I immediately imagined going to visit Ty Mawr and taking some burka-clad Muslim women with me. That floored me for starters; as I pictured the scenario, I realized I would be the only one *not* in a veil of some sort. Enough said. But I couldn't help enjoying the picture of the convent, all cosy against the drizzle of Welsh rain, the sisters sitting around in the library handing out tea and slices of cake to their veiled visitors, chatting away with them. More than anything I knew their response would be what it had been when I'd met them all those years before: a smile, and open welcoming arms, beckoning the newcomer to join them. So I started with that – well, the smile at least. Every time I met the eye of a Muslim woman on the bus or tube or on Oxford Street I decided I would smile at her.

It's a hard thing to do when you feel stupid, and I did feel stupid. It was kind of ridiculous and could have been badly misinterpreted, especially since I felt I really had to force it to begin with and probably looked like I was giving a weird wince. But the image of the nuns' tea party stuck with me – a fearless sisterhood of women – and it was a picture I could believe in. I wanted to overcome the distance between sisters on different sides of the religious fence.

When the girls arrived at the London College of Fashion on the first day, I was told by one of the interfaith facilitators that none of the girls from Islamic schools studied art or music; these subjects had been removed from their timetable.

FLASH

'^$%! *£% @$*&'

Breathe...

"OK, so let's see how they get on with some sketching." I handed out slim sticks of bamboo and small pots of coloured ink and set a clothed mannequin in front of them to copy.

They were a marvel.

How did these girls learn to draw and paint like this if they weren't taught? Which in my head sounded more like an indignant yelp of *"It's criminal for anyone to rob these girls of their chance to be creative."* But then I looked again at Aliya, the robed young teacher in front of me, and thought how much she had done to get these girls here in the first place. She and others had been working for months, smoothing the way with school authorities and parents and the girls themselves, to make this possible. The result was magnificent, and I wanted to meet the girls in their enthusiasm and do everything possible to enable them to make the most of the opportunity.

But I was in for a rough ride. We were taking a spacious, reflective look at our stories and our identity. For these girls their art, their poetry and their fashion designs all came back to modesty. They had been well schooled and I was intrigued by the frequent partnership of the words "beauty" and "modesty" in the annotations around their designs. Their veiling was carried out with utter self-respect. If a man came to visit the studio, gentle nudges were given, faces would turn aside and veils would be quietly let down to fully cover their faces. Then there was the tall girl who even wore gloves to cover her hands, whose elegance and self-possession were evident, even under layers of flowing black fabric.

These girls weren't telling me the story that I had believed about them. As I sat alongside, helping them to reflect on their drawings and make connections between their history, their faith and their identity, I realized they were rewriting a part of my story. It wasn't just a privilege to have these girls come and attend the summer school; it was a privilege to encounter them, to listen to them. They opened up about the prejudice they felt others held towards them because of their dress, and their stories moved me.

And on the second day we were to see these reactions unfold before our eyes. We were sharing the small campus of studios with another summer school, this one attended by eighteen-year-old school leavers. So, when we took our lunch out into the small grassy area outside the cafeteria and collided with the older, hot-pants-and-skinny-vest-wearing students, it was the stuff caption competitions are made of. Our girls needed to let off steam, but they weren't taking any robes off in the process. So, as a teenage version of "What's the Time Mr Wolf?" ensued and veiled girls raced and shouted and black robes billowed, the other tutors and I sat back to watch the reaction of the older students.

Having just listened as the girls had told us how keenly they felt the judgement and misperceptions of strangers because of their religious clothing, I wasn't surprised by what I saw. While our girls continued to laugh and race, the mouths of the older girls were covered in hands as whispers passed back and forth; quiet stares gave way to sidelong looks of snide incredulity. It was the kind of reaction that anyone might have on crash-landing unexpectedly in someone else's subculture, but I felt protectiveness for "my" girls, as I was beginning to see them. Over the small lawn I caught the eye of Aliya, but her calm smile told me those instincts were premature. It wasn't our girls who were acting insecure; there was no evidence right now that they doubted themselves because of how they were dressed or perceived. I wished the same were the case for the girls perching on the walls, whispering and looking on.

Throughout their art, their reflective notes and poetry and even in their stalking of Mr Wolf, it was evident that these fourteen- and fifteen-year-olds had discovered something of what it means to inhabit their own place in the world. Their way of seeing themselves was not in comparison with celebrities or cover girls or any other image of beauty plastered onto our cultural wallpaper. Their hijabs were like a pre-emptive strike on the temptation to derive their value from the approval of men in the way Western women were persuaded to by marketing companies and celebrity obsessions. These girls leaned into their self-image as modest and therefore beautiful, and they derived great strength and purpose from it. But if I was hoping to hear them say that they were made to wear it then I was going to be disappointed. The only hint I detected was when they talked about wishing their hijabs were more colourful and had prettier designs. I made a mental note to invite Novice Joy the next time we ran this summer school. The following day one of the girls arrived in a bright pink hijab embroidered with tiny white flowers. "This course is making me feel differently about what I wear, and this pink one says what I feel." She beamed shyly.

And yet they were instructed to wear it. No matter how much they insisted it was their choice and they were freely choosing to embrace their covering, it was all the same a cultural construct of beauty and worth valued by their world; just a different one from the one I had listened to when I was their age.

Theirs was upheld by elders, imams, fathers and mothers and peers; mine by a cacophony of bullies, preachers, godly wives and supermodels. But all of us, whether hot-pant-wearing kafir or Islamic schoolgirls in niqabs, were carving our niche into a pathway already hewn for us, whether through the force of religion or of liberal capitalism. And all of us would trip and fall again and again as we tried to match up to the perfection set for us because each of us would, in our own way, mistake that contrived perfection for the kind of love that could dispel our shame and doubt and fear.

On the final morning I sat at a table with four girls as they told me about the kind of Islamic love songs they were allowed to listen to. Songs whose lyrics were reminiscent of the choruses we sang at Bible camp about our love for God. I wondered if the choruses we sang about being in love with Jesus would translate to Mohammed; I smiled to myself at the possibility that that's what they had been singing over the fence at Islamic Youth Camp all those years ago.

But even if our desire was directed towards very different leaders, it soon became clear that they weren't so unlike me at the age of fourteen. Their chatter, which had begun with love, soon crossed over into the fears they had about judgement and punishment.

"The judgement I really don't want is the ultimate one where you get buried in a pit with snakes and everything. That's at the end of the world", the girl next to me explained. My knowledge of the Islamic version of Judgement Day was zero but, going on past experience, I felt I had a handle on just how troubled this girl could be. Absorbed in colouring the layers of her dress design, she talked to me about the three levels of punishment and how she hoped she would never experience eternal banishment into this dark, snake-ridden pit. Underneath her robes and piety she was just as worried as I had been about failing and falling into the wrathful hands of God.

As I listened to her, it struck me that a tea party with the nuns might be a very good idea. To introduce them to the sisters who had been more like mothers to me and who had the strength to love, in the name of God, everything that people brought to them. But there would be no such Welsh field trip; these girls just had me and the other facilitators, so right now it was down to me to be the older sister, able to hear and hold all the fear she wanted to name. By the time she had finished describing these punishments her colouring motion had become languid, as if her energy had drained away.

I asked her to imagine she had a child.

She nodded.

"And imagine that child began to rebel against you and act in a way that you'd taught her not to."

More nodding.

"Then this child begins not just acting out but actually seems to turn against you and reject you. How would you feel about your child, do you think?"

"I'd feel sad and I'd want to do all I could to bring her back to me."

"Yes. I think you would do everything you could to bring your child back to a good relationship with you."

She nodded. "I would."

"I think that's how Allah feels towards you. Unstoppable love."

She smiled in recognition.

"And from everything you've told me you want to be in a good place with Allah …"

"Yes."

"So it sounds like you and Allah are after the same thing then?"

She smiled at me, her enthusiasm returning in the vigorous nod of her head.

"You know, we're both going to mess it up, no matter how much we want to do the right thing? Even though you're wearing the right clothes you'll get it wrong at times."

She sighed and nodded.

"But if Allah is Allah then we can trust that we'll be met by mercy and kindness and it's not down to us to be perfect on our own."

"That would be idolatry."

"Yeah, it would, like we were saying we are OK on our own and we don't need love and understanding and forgiveness."

"Mmmm", she agreed.

"So that pit of judgement with all the snakes in it that you mentioned: don't think about that – it'll just sow fear. Think about having a heart that stays open for Allah to pour His love into."

The Jewish interfaith facilitator turned round from her table and nodded, smiling. "Amen."

That afternoon as the girls presented their finished designs I read an inscription on a piece of fabric:

I thought only Muslim women were modest and I thought only modest women could be truly beautiful. Now I know that's not true. I know that women can be faithful and devout and modest even without veils, even outside of Islam, and that is beautiful.

Epilogue

If I had been designing an outfit for the Empty Hanger that week I wonder what my storyboard would have looked like as I gathered the fabric of my beliefs, experiences and hopes into a design. We'd asked students to bring with them an object that was significant for them as a starting point for their designs. And so I would have brought the wooden cross, carved for me by Sister Clare when I became an Associate of the Community at Ty Mawr. On one side it had etched the shape of an open-armed figure; it captured entirely the fearless posture the sisters embodied, but it was probably meant to be Jesus on the cross, or the resurrected Jesus showing he has overcome failure, guilt, fear and death with Life. Showing that love can clothe and transform all that we are.

I thought about all I was, but we can never really observe ourselves; we only see ourselves reflected in the beauty we recognize in others and in the things that bring us to life and cause us to lose ourselves in a vision beyond. We catch glimpses in the wounds that make us wince when bruised by others, and how they remind us that it wasn't meant to be like this; that we're not yet Home.

So, if I had been designing my outfit for the Empty Hanger, there would have been, first, a trail of falling leaves cut from the fabric of a damson suede mini-skirt, from the black plastic bin-liner of my underwater blob costume, from the insipid blue gingham of a student nurse's uniform and from ugly, black, clerical polycotton.

And above it, around the template of a naked figure, would be a tunic made from pieces of tartan trousers that had once belonged to a punk boy, from a nun's wimple and a pink-and-white hijab; and a white plastic dog-collar, smudged with red lipstick.

Acknowledgments

Massive thanks goes to a whole bunch of people who in their different ways enabled, persuaded, cajoled and encouraged me to write this book.

Caroline Chartres, who waited years for me to get my act together and write it all down – thank you for all your support, patience, wit and vision along the way … and for enduring all the early attempts to tell it: it was therapeutic, for me at least.

Rosalind Waters, who relived so many of these events far more often than she wanted to; willingly reading and re-reading countless passages, who prescribed me tea/champagne/gin at what I felt were very inopportune moments when I was busy having an authorial crisis, and who generally encouraged me to keep going. Thank you.

Enormous thanks go to Elizabeth Gowing who is one of the most awesome women I know, and who became my writing buddy even though it meant reading an awful lot about God and not enough about the adventures she was hoping to hear more of, and whose brilliance has inspired me in writing and so very much beyond. Time for some new pebbles?

Similarly heartfelt thanks to Emma Karran who so generously gave time to remember many of these events and more, and who with great wisdom and humour helped me piece the memories and conversations back together ….

It was a privilege to have Robert Wilton involved in the writing process, and I am full of thanks for his readiness to make comments and suggestions, and to celebrate any and every milestone that could be found along the way. There are, hopefully, many more to come.

Thanks also to Jamie Birkett, Kim Storry and Ellen Williams, and to Matthew Waters, Jeff Stuckey, Vicky Harper, Chris MacGregor, Siona Stockel, Merryn Gamba, Caroline Bruce, Derek Mills, Helen Hawkins and Charles Hawkins, who each in their own way offered much-appreciated support and input.

I have loved the poem *Muddy* for a long, long time, and I am hugely grateful to Patrick Hobbs for letting me reproduce it at the beginning of this book – it really says it all.

These acknowledgements wouldn't be complete without thanking Alastair Jepson, who has championed me at every step, and encourages me to get up and keep going at every hurdle over which I trip.

Joachim Woerner, without whom this story would have been a sad and truncated version of what it is and probably not worth telling, thank you for everything.

Thanks also go to Vanessa Bruch, the Catalan equivalent of Mary Poppins, without whom this book could not have been written. Thank you for becoming part of our family and for being the love of Raphael's life while I was locked away for hours on end.

Dad, you've been unwavering in your encouragement to write this story down and I am so grateful for that. Thank you for all you have done to make this the story that I can tell.

Nick, I am so grateful for everything you have done to support and encourage me in writing this book. I hope the full extent of my fundamentalist childhood will be a shock from which you can recover! Thank you for knowing when to laugh and when not to …

Finally, having spent most of these writing months locked away in my study ignoring my friends and sending only the occasional text blaming The Book for my absence, I am thoroughly glad to have the chance now to thank – for all their encouragement and enthusiasm, and for keeping my number in their contacts list – Jane Addis, Juliet Barwell, Sal Bermejo, Chris Blockley, Tamsin Bond, Sasha Gibson, Jenny Lincoln-Jones, Erica Wax, Tori Welsh, Kate Wiggs and Ben Wright …

Copyright Permissions